# Benjamin Harrison

# Charles W. Calhoun

# Benjamin Harrison

**THE AMERICAN PRESIDENTS**

ARTHUR M. SCHLESINGER, JR., GENERAL EDITOR

Times Books

HENRY HOLT AND COMPANY, NEW YORK

Times Books
Henry Holt and Company, LLC
*Publishers since 1866*
175 Fifth Avenue
New York, New York 10010
www.henryholt.com

Henry Holt® is a registered trademark of Henry Holt and Company, LLC.

LIBRARY OF CONGRESS CATALOGING-IN-PUBLICATION DATA

Calhoun, Charles W. (Charles William), 1948–
Benjamin Harrison / Charles W. Calhoun.—1st ed.
p. cm.—(The American presidents series)
Includes bibliographical references (p.   ) and index.
ISBN-13: 978-0-8050-6952-5
ISBN-10: 0-8050-6952-6
1. Harrison, Benjamin, 1833–1901.   2. Presidents—United States—
Biography.   3. United States—Politics and government—1889–1893.   I. Title.
II. American presidents series (Times Books (Firm))
E702.C35 2005
973.8'6'092—dc22
[B]                                                          2004063778

First Edition 2005

Printed in the United States of America
1   3   5   7   9   10   8   6   4   2

*To Ben Walker*

# Contents

# Editor's Note

THE AMERICAN PRESIDENCY

The president is the central player in the American political order. That would seem to contradict the intentions of the Founding Fathers. Remembering the horrid example of the British monarchy, they invented a separation of powers in order, as Justice Brandeis later put it, "to preclude the exercise of arbitrary power." Accordingly, they divided the government into three allegedly equal and coordinate branches—the executive, the legislative, and the judiciary.

But a system based on the tripartite separation of powers has an inherent tendency toward inertia and stalemate. One of the three branches must take the initiative if the system is to move. The executive branch alone is structurally capable of taking that initiative. The Founders must have sensed this when they accepted Alexander Hamilton's proposition in the Seventieth Federalist that "energy in the executive is a leading character in the definition of good government." They thus envisaged a strong president—but within an equally strong system of constitutional accountability. (The term *imperial presidency* arose in the 1970s to describe the situation when the balance between power and accountability is upset in favor of the executive.)

The American system of self-government thus comes to focus in the presidency—"the vital place of action in the system," as Woodrow Wilson put it. Henry Adams, himself the great-grandson and grandson of presidents as well as the most brilliant of American historians, said that the American president "resembles the commander of a ship at sea. He must have a helm to grasp, a course to steer, a port to seek." The men in the White House (thus far only men, alas) in steering their chosen courses have shaped our destiny as a nation.

Biography offers an easy education in American history, rendering the past more human, more vivid, more intimate, more accessible, more connected to ourselves. Biography reminds us that presidents are not supermen. They are human beings too, worrying about decisions, attending to wives and children, juggling balls in the air, and putting on their pants one leg at a time. Indeed, as Emerson contended, "There is properly no history; only biography."

Presidents serve us as inspirations, and they also serve us as warnings. They provide bad examples as well as good. The nation, the Supreme Court has said, has "no right to expect that it will always have wise and humane rulers, sincerely attached to the principles of the Constitution. Wicked men, ambitious of power, with hatred of liberty and contempt of law, may fill the place once occupied by Washington and Lincoln."

The men in the White House express the ideals and the values, the frailties and the flaws of the voters who send them there. It is altogether natural that we should want to know more about the virtues and the vices of the fellows we have elected to govern us. As we know more about them, we will know more about ourselves. The French political philosopher Joseph de Maistre said, "Every nation has the government it deserves."

At the start of the twenty-first century, forty-two men have made it to the Oval Office. (George W. Bush is counted our forty-third president because Grover Cleveland, who served nonconsecutive terms, is counted twice.) Of the parade of presidents, a dozen or so lead the polls periodically conducted by historians and political scientists. What makes a great president?

Great presidents possess, or are possessed by, a vision of an ideal America. Their passion, as they grasp the helm, is to set the ship of state on the right course toward the port they seek. Great presidents also have a deep psychic connection with the needs, anxieties, dreams of people. "I do not believe," said Wilson, "that any man can lead who does not act . . . under the impulse of a profound sympathy with those whom he leads—a sympathy which is insight—an insight which is of the heart rather than of the intellect."

"All of our great presidents," said Franklin D. Roosevelt, "were leaders of thought at a time when certain ideas in the life of the nation had to be clarified." So Washington incarnated the idea of federal union, Jefferson and Jackson the idea of democracy, Lincoln union and freedom, Cleveland rugged honesty. Theodore Roosevelt and Wilson, said FDR, were both "moral leaders, each in his own way and his own time, who used the presidency as a pulpit."

To succeed, presidents must not only have a port to seek but they must convince Congress and the electorate that it is a port worth seeking. Politics in a democracy is ultimately an educational process, an adventure in persuasion and consent. Every president stands in Theodore Roosevelt's bully pulpit.

The greatest presidents in the scholars' rankings, Washington, Lincoln, and Franklin Roosevelt, were leaders who confronted and overcame the republic's greatest crises. Crisis widens presidential opportunities for bold and imaginative action. But it does not guarantee presidential greatness. The crisis of secession did not spur Buchanan or the crisis of depression spur Hoover to creative leadership. Their inadequacies in the face of crisis allowed Lincoln and the second Roosevelt to show the difference individuals make to history. Still, even in the absence of first-order crisis, forceful and persuasive presidents—Jefferson, Jackson, James K. Polk, Theodore Roosevelt, Ronald Reagan—are able to impose their own priorities on the country.

The diverse drama of the presidency offers a fascinating set of tales. Biographies of American presidents constitute a chronicle of wisdom and folly, nobility and pettiness, courage and cunning, forthrightness and deceit, quarrel and consensus. The turmoil perennially swirling around the White House illuminates the heart of the American democracy.

It is the aim of the American Presidents series to present the grand panorama of our chief executives in volumes compact enough for the busy reader, lucid enough for the student, authoritative enough for the scholar. Each volume offers a distillation of character and career. I hope that these lives will give readers some understanding of the pitfalls and potentialities of the presidency and also of the responsibilities of citizenship. Truman's famous sign—"The buck stops here"—tells only half the story. Citizens cannot escape the ultimate responsibility. It is in the voting booth, not on the presidential desk, that the buck finally stops.

—Arthur M. Schlesinger, Jr.

# Introduction

In *The Education*, Henry Adams wrote that Benjamin Harrison "was an excellent President, a man of ability and force; perhaps the best President the Republican Party had put forward since Lincoln's death." Yet, Adams added, when Harrison was up for reelection in 1892, he "felt a shade of preference for President Cleveland."[1] The comment said as much about Adams as it did about Harrison, but it also symbolizes the strange ambivalence, a compound of success and failure, that marked the presidency of Benjamin Harrison. The twenty-third president racked up a long list of accomplishments in the White House, a good many more than his predecessor Grover Cleveland, but at the end of Harrison's term, the nation turned him out and brought back the man he had defeated four years earlier. How can one explain such success and such failure?

As a public man and president, Harrison enjoyed a wealth of assets. He was the scion of a venerable family of leaders, and his grandfather had attained the White House forty years earlier. He possessed a keen intellect and was well and broadly educated. He was a devout Christian who took seriously his calling to do good in the world. His training as a lawyer made him a master at penetrating analysis and irresistible persuasion. He had a seemingly boundless capacity for hard work. He understood his nation's history, its problems, and its promise. He had seen war firsthand and had returned home with a deepened sense of the meaning and purposes of leadership. He harbored a philosophy of government that emphasized possibilities more than restraints. He was an astute political strategist, with a profound comprehension of his countrymen's attitudes and aspirations. He was a superb orator, who could give five speeches a day, each one original, different, extemporaneous, and affecting.

All these gifts aided Harrison's climb to the presidency and served him well in the work of governing. But Harrison's victory in 1888 (as well as his defeat in 1892) also grew out of the particular circumstances that defined the political universe in which he operated. During Harrison's time, the two major parties stood at almost exact equilibrium in the national electorate. This was not a Republican era, as some traditional accounts suggest, but instead one in which Democrats and Republicans were nearly equal in their support nationwide. A considerable portion of the Democrats' strength came from the Solid South, where most Republican African Americans could not vote. For their part, the Republicans could rely almost as surely on winning substantial majorities in several states in the Northeast and upper Midwest. But neither the Republican nor the Democratic bloc held enough electoral votes by itself to win the presidency, and any given election turned on the outcome in a handful of "doubtful" states, principally New York and Indiana.

This equilibrium in party strength tended to magnify the importance of party management and organization and to elevate the power of state party bosses, especially in those doubtful states. If a powerful state leader were for some reason "off" the presidential nominee, a decision by him and his associates to sit out the campaign could prove fatal to the nominee's chances. Similarly, when presidents won elections narrowly, party bosses were quick to claim that their efforts provided the winning edge and to demand patronage recognition as their reward.

This political equipoise also moved party leaders to handle issues with care out of fear of alienating some group or interest and thereby jeopardizing victory. Even so, Republicans and Democrats differed sharply over matters of public policy and offered voters real choices at the polls. Benjamin Harrison and other Republicans, Hamiltonians at heart, placed greater stress on government activism, especially at the national level, with the primary aim of fostering economic development. They welcomed the nation's burgeoning industrialization and believed the federal government should assist the process. Over time, the protective tariff emerged as the centerpiece of the Republicans' economic program. Most Democrats, on the other hand, clung to their party's Jeffersonian belief in small government and states' rights. They criticized elements in the Republicans' program as favoring special interests. With its low-tariff wing from the agrarian, largely preindustrial South still looming large, the Democratic Party continued its decades-old opposition to tariff protectionism.

In 1888 the elements of this political universe worked in Harrison's favor. He hailed from the doubtful state of Indiana and boasted an impressive record as a soldier, lawyer, senator, and party spokesman—both of which helped him win the Republican nomination. During the campaign, Republican state managers, eager to win back the White House and its bounteous patronage, swung the party apparatus behind Harrison's cause. And in the summer and fall, the nominee himself proved to be the most eloquent and effective advocate of the party's philosophy, which he articulated in a brilliant front-porch campaign. Harrison lost the popular vote but won the White House, as had John Quincy Adams and Rutherford B. Hayes before him and as George W. Bush would do in 2000. Cleveland's popular-vote edge came from lopsided Democratic majorities in the Deep South. Harrison, however, won New York, Indiana, and a majority in the electoral college. Moreover, he carried with him to Washington a Republican Congress.

Once in power, Harrison and his party governed energetically. On the domestic front, Harrison was a legislative president far more than most other nineteenth-century chief executives. He employed a variety of means to achieve his ends: veto threats to influence the shape of legislation, well-timed messages and public statements to garner support, and informal dinners at the White House and other consultations with congressmen to push them in the right direction. Harrison's first Congress passed an impressive array of measures, which included the McKinley Tariff Act, the Sherman Anti-Trust Act, the Sherman Silver Purchase Act, the Dependent Pension Act, the Forest Reserve Act, and many others. In addition, Harrison was the central figure in conducting the nation's foreign affairs, not merely in setting the broad outlines of policy but also in the delicate work of direct diplomacy. He shepherded the nation through several medium-sized crises, presided over a substantial expansion of the navy, and pursued an active program to increase the nation's trade.

More than all his predecessors, Harrison carried the presidency to the people. He traveled widely, including a cross-country tour, and spoke often, explaining his and his party's vision to the nation. Harrison regarded himself as a born-again Christian, and in his rhetoric, he frequently turned to civil religious themes that emphasized republicanism, equality of opportunity, and order. He saw the nation as on a mission to demonstrate the merits of free representative government—a mission whose success rested on a contented and prosperous citizenry. "I do not know how our institutions could endure," he declared, "unless we so conduct our public affairs and society that every man who is sober and industrious shall be able to make a good, comfortable living and lay something aside for old age and evil days; to have hope in his heart and better prospects for his children. That is the strength of American institutions. Whatever promotes that I want to favor."[2] What promoted that, he argued, was the Republican Party's policies.

By any reasonable account, it would seem that, as Henry Adams put it, Harrison was "an excellent President." Then why did voters reject him in 1892? To some extent, they rejected him because he had succeeded too well. In 1890 the Republicans lost overwhelmingly in the midterm congressional elections. Their activist agenda offended and perhaps frightened many essentially conservative voters who held on to the traditional American notion that good government meant limited government. Disenchantment was wide-spread among farmers and laborers, and Harrison was unable to convince them that his party's policies served their ultimate best interest. Nonetheless, he continued unabashedly to defend his party's accomplishments, and he paid the price. In addition, Harrison found it impossible to satisfy the demands for patronage recognition that swamped him after taking office. Although he labored long hours over appointments, he never had enough to go around, and resentment built among party bosses. Nor did Harrison's introverted, sometimes self-righteous personality equip him with the skills necessary to smooth hurt feelings among men whose help he needed. Even the nonboss Henry Adams, miffed at the administration's neglect of some of his friends, grumbled that he felt "irritation at seeing how President Harrison dealt his cards."[3] Harrison did manage to win renomination, but in the fall of 1892, many party leaders showed far less enthusiasm and performed far less campaign work than they had in 1888. Finally, in 1892 Harrison's wife was quite ill, and she died two weeks before the election. Her illness and death prevented Harrison from playing the sort of highly visible and effective role he had taken in the 1888 campaign. The conditions of the political universe that had allowed Harrison to win the presidency now worked against him, the balance in the party equilibrium shifted, and he lost his second election to Cleveland, the man he had defeated four years earlier.

Harrison is often dismissed simply as the man who occupied the White House between Cleveland's two terms. Yet, in the evolution and growth of the presidency, Harrison's term pointed the way of the future far more than did Cleveland's. Whereas Harrison had skillfully worked closely with his party's leaders in Congress, Cleveland's second term found the president locked in frustrating combat with members of his own party on Capitol Hill. Whereas Harrison had traveled freely among his constituents and worked well with the press, Cleveland had grown so unpopular by the end of his term as to be holed up in the White House a virtual prisoner. William McKinley, Cleveland's successor, picked up, in a sense, where Harrison left off. As a leader in Congress during Harrison's term, McKinley had witnessed firsthand the techniques Harrison used to achieve his ends. As president himself, McKinley applied many of these same techniques, though he did so with a warmer personal sensitivity and greater political skill. As a result, many modern scholars regard McKinley as the nation's first modern president. That may be true, but a careful review of Harrison's performance demonstrates that McKinley and his successors owed much to the example set by Benjamin Harrison.

After he left the White House, Harrison returned to Indianapolis, resumed the practice of law, found love and married again, shunned any thought of returning to public life, and harbored no doubts that he had fulfilled his duty as president faithfully and well and to the greater benefit of the nation. During the disastrous term of his successor, many of his countrymen came to agree with him and to regret his and their loss.

# 1

---

# "A Hard-Earned Loaf"

Few American presidents have descended from lines more distinguished for public service than the one that produced Benjamin Harrison. Beginning in the seventeenth century, a succession of five Benjamin Harrisons figured prominently in the development of colonial Virginia. The last one held extensive tracts of land, the jewel of which was Berkeley plantation, on the James River. Benjamin Harrison V represented Virginia in the Continental Congress, headed the committee that reported the Declaration of Independence, and rounded out his political career as governor of the new state of Virginia.[1]

Benjamin V's son, William Henry Harrison, added even greater luster to the family escutcheon. Born at Berkeley three years before his father signed the Declaration, William Henry entered the army at age eighteen. Posted to duty in the Indian struggles in the old Northwest, he soon distinguished himself both as a soldier and a politician. In 1811, while serving as governor of Indiana Territory, he destroyed the Shawnee chief Tecumseh's project for a defensive Indian confederation at the Battle of Tippecanoe Creek. As a general in the War of 1812, William Henry Harrison won an even more significant victory over the British at the Battle of Thames River in October 1813. It was, however, Tippecanoe that more prominently entered into political lore and lent its victor his indelible sobriquet.

After the war, Harrison settled on a large farm in North Bend, near Cincinnati, Ohio, but in the ensuing decade, his financial and political fortunes suffered ups and downs. In 1828 President John Quincy Adams sent him as the first American minister to the new Republic of Colombia, but in less than a year he headed home, a victim of the "rotation in office" (or spoils system) launched by Andrew Jackson. He returned to North Bend, and, with scant hope for preferment in the changing political climate, he accepted appointment as clerk of the Hamilton County court to supplement his farm income.

Harrison's emergence from this political desuetude partook of the miraculous. In the mid-1830s Jackson's opponents adopted the name *Whig* and began organizing a campaign to defeat Vice President Martin Van Buren for the presidential succession. Not yet jelled as a national party in 1836, the Whigs fielded three regional candidates—Harrison, Daniel Webster of Massachusetts, and Hugh Lawson White of Tennessee—against the Democrat Van Buren in hopes of throwing the contest into the House of Representatives. Many turned to Harrison, a popular westerner whose military exploits echoed Old Hickory's. Though the strategy failed, Harrison emerged as a Whig of national appeal and, four years later, the party nominated him for president. The rollicking ballyhoo of the ensuing "Hard Cider and Log Cabin" campaign touted the Virginia-born gentleman as an apt representative, if not actual specimen, of the common man. The Whigs also hammered away at the prevailing economic depression during the reign of "Martin Van Ruin," and in the end, hard times as much as "Hard Cider" put Harrison in the White House.[2]

On March 4, 1841, William Henry Harrison took the oath of office as the nation's ninth president. Seven-year-old Benjamin Harrison was not on hand for the event, but it was just as well, for his sixty-eight-year-old grandfather took an hour and a half to deliver the longest inaugural address in history to a crowd huddled against a frigid northeast wind. None too well to begin with and hounded to exhaustion by office-hungry Whigs, the new chief executive took a chill in late March. He soon contracted pneumonia and grew progressively worse under his doctors' "care," which included bleeding, blistering, and quantities of arsenic. He died on April 4, one month into his term.[3]

Back in Ohio, William Henry Harrison's third son, John Scott Harrison, had years earlier assumed the management of the North Bend farm. Born in 1804, John Scott had briefly aspired to a medical career, but he was essentially a farmer his whole life. Although he dabbled in politics, The Point, the six-hundred-acre farm he had received from his father, formed the source of his livelihood. Prosperity eluded him, yet he produced enough to feed, clothe, and house his large family, which grew to include nine offspring. Chronically in debt, he was willing to skirt the edge of financial ruin to provide his children a good education.[4]

Benjamin Harrison was born August 20, 1833, in his grandfather's house at North Bend. His mother, Elizabeth Irwin, Scott Harrison's second wife, was descended from Scottish immigrants who had achieved a comfortable life in America, if less distinction than the Harrison forebears. Elizabeth was raised in the strict Presbyterian faith and took a leading part in the religious and moral training of her children.[5]

Despite his father's financial troubles, Benjamin enjoyed a happy childhood. He did his share of work on the farm but had his share of play as well. Early on, he developed an abiding fondness for hunting and fishing, pursuits that became his favorite forms of recreation during his crowded adult life. He liked to read too, and for this appetite his grandfather's well-stocked library was a godsend. There volumes of ancient history, American history, and biography, as well as Walter Scott's Waverley novels and other tales of adventure transported him beyond the semifrontier of the Ohio Valley. At his mother's urging, he also read Bunyan's *Pilgrim's Progress*.[6]

This latter exercise fit naturally into the devotional duties that marked life in the Harrison household. In the era of the Second Great Awakening, religion loomed large for the Harrisons as for

most Americans. Daily prayer and Bible reading nurtured conviction between Sundays, which generally saw the family headed some
distance to church. When bad weather prevented the trip, they still
kept the Sabbath conscientiously, shunning worldly activity, the
better to contemplate the gift of God's grace. Later in life, Harrison
remembered the awe he felt at the nightly ritual of his mother
withdrawing from the family circle to commune alone with her
heavenly Father. She bore as much solicitude for her children's
souls as for her own; she once wrote the teenaged Benjamin, "I pray
for you daily that you may be kept from sinning and straying from
the paths of duty." As a grown man of faith and responsibility, he
made this prayer his own.[7]

Benjamin's formal education began in a rough log cabin erected
on his father's property. There a succession of tutors delivered the
fundamentals of primary instruction to the Harrison children, their
cousins, and other children from nearby farms. The first of these
teachers later remembered that "Ben was the brightest of the family, and even when five years old was determined to go ahead in
everything."[8]

In the fall of 1847, John Scott Harrison scraped together the
money to send fourteen-year-old Benjamin and his older brother
Irwin to Farmers' College, an institution near Cincinnati that offered
both preparatory and college-level instruction. There Ben came
under the powerful influence of Professor Robert Hamilton Bishop,
a Presbyterian minister and distinguished educator who taught history and political economy. Former students who had gone on to
serve in Congress provided Bishop with a steady stream of government reports that he passed on to students as bases for their essays
and recitations. By this device, he cultivated not only his students'
powers of analysis and composition but also their understanding of
contemporary political issues and governance.[9]

Bishop combined those lessons with care for his students' moral
and religious development, instilling in them the importance of
stewardship and social responsibility in their journey toward salva-

tion. In one of his compositions for Bishop, Benjamin wrote that under God's watchful eye, "one[']s ability shall be the measure of his accountability, hence as persons increase in wealth and their power of doing good increases in the same ratio[,] they will be held accountable for all the good they might have done."[10]

In an essay comparing the life of savage and civilized men, Benjamin argued that a "good criterion" for judging the "true state of society" was how it treated women, for women "are appreciated in proportion as society is advanced." In America, he wrote, a woman "is considered as a superior being, and in the eyes of many as an angel. This, however, is the case only when we behold them through the telescope of love."[11]

These truths occurred to him not merely as a result of abstract rumination; at Farmers' College the teenaged Benjamin Harrison had fallen in love. The object of his affection was Caroline Lavinia Scott, the daughter of John W. Scott, another Presbyterian minister, who taught chemistry and physics at the college and who also ran a school for girls in Cincinnati. During the spring of 1848, the diminutive freshman—slight of build with pale skin and thin blond hair—began to call at the Scott house. He soon took notice of the petite, slightly plump Carrie with her kindly eyes and profusion of exquisite brown hair. Before long, the serious-minded, ambitious boy found that he much enjoyed the company of this warmhearted and sympathetic girl, ten months his senior, whose vivacity and playful sense of humor drew him out of his solemn introspection. Their friendship quickly ripened into romance.

Within a year, however, Professor Scott moved his girls' school to Oxford, Ohio, more than twenty miles away. Not long afterward, Benjamin turned to thoughts of transferring to Miami University, also at Oxford. Despite a personal plea from the president of Farmers' to stay until graduation, Benjamin matriculated as a junior at Miami in the fall of 1850. This was a time of emotional turmoil for the seventeen-year-old boy. During the summer, he had witnessed the death of his beloved mother and two younger siblings. "How such events should impress us with the necessity of making our peace with God!" he wrote to Bishop, whom he asked to let him know "whenever you may see anything in my course which you deem reprehensible." His heavy heart would welcome renewed steady company with Carrie at Oxford.[12]

Harrison flourished at Miami. Well prepared by Bishop, he soon distinguished himself for his intelligence and his hard work. As one fellow student recalled, he "excelled in political economy and history" and "never seemed to regard life as a joke nor the opportunities for advancement as subjects for sport." His manifest abilities won him election as president of the Union Literary Society. The society's training in public speaking and argumentation proved nearly as useful as his formal course work. He honed skills at debate and extemporaneous speaking, which served him all his life.[13]

Harrison's essays and speeches at Farmers' and Miami often focused on political subjects, both current events and broader philosophical themes. Although his ideas remained inchoate, they exhibited his fundamental sense that politics had a larger purpose than party advantage and that public service should aim toward bettering the condition of men and nations. Harrison saluted Henry Clay's Compromise of 1850 as a noble work that steered between sectional extremes and saved the country. He denounced intemperance as "a moral, social, and political curse" and defended the power of legislatures to check the depredations of demon rum. In the realm of political economy, he saw commerce as "absolutely necessary to the welfare, happiness, and prosperity of every nation," but he also argued against a government trade policy that made England the "workshop of America." Instead, he said, "our manufactures should be strengthened and built up." In reaction to the liberal uprisings that convulsed Europe at midcentury, Harrison maintained that the United States should exert its influence on other countries not by direct intervention but by example. "Our mission is not to impose our peculiar institutions upon other nations by physical force or diplomatic treachery but rather by internal peace and prosperity to solve the problem of self-government and reconcile democratic freedom with national stability."[14]

Dominated by Presbyterian ministers, Miami hosted frequent religious revivals. At one such meeting during his first year, Harrison answered the call and entered into formal association with the church. Given his training at home, the move was not unexpected, but his father was nonetheless delighted. Nor was the act one of mere momentary youthful exuberance. Harrison remained a faithful communicant for the rest of his life.

For some time, the anxious and ambitious youth weighed entering the ministry against becoming a lawyer. In the end, he chose the law, but that did not mean he had turned his back on doing God's work. In a speech to fellow students, he lamented the seeming dominance of scoundrels in the legal profession but denied the "proposition that no honest or pious man can practice law with success." "Fellow Christians," he said, "if you adopt this Prof[ession], let me effectively entreat you to remember that you are to do all to the glory of God." Moreover, he believed that the profession of politics, no less than the law, should be imbued with moral energy and purpose.

Strange as it may appear there are those who deem their Christian professions at variance with their civil duties, as if the church were the only institution of God's own planting, the only sphere in which they are called to act, whose narrow minds can grasp but one class of duties and but poorly apprehend even those. Yet such is a prevailing notion among many Christians who glory in the shameful boast, "I'm no politician." "I have nothing to do with politics." Such should remember that civil society is no less an institution of God than the Church, that society can in no sense exist without government, and that man is the instrumentality appointed to administer this government. . . . The church, as a church, can take no part in the affairs of state but individual members of the church as embodying the only true morality and as members of civil society, owe to that society of which they form an integral part certain duties for the neglect of which God will not hold them guiltless.[15]

Harrison took third honors at his graduation in June 1852. While classmates devoted their commencement orations to subjects such as the death of Socrates and the "Poetry of Religion," Harrison analyzed a question of government social policy in his lecture, "The Poor of England." He began by asking how the old England of virtuous and self-sufficient yeomen had degenerated into a nation with widespread destitution and some eight million paupers. The "common answer," he said, was to blame the country's poor laws, the system whereby the parish government paid a dole to supplement the insufficient wages of workers. He repeated the accepted wisdom that such a scheme had the effect of "sapping the life's blood of individual energy and encouraging indolence." But, he said, far worse in "grossness and deformity," the system allowed employers to shirk their responsibility to their workers and reduce their wages. Thus, the wealthy employer paid a relatively insignificant poor rate, or tax, that left him his "princely magnificence," while "his operatives are paupers and their poverty places them entirely within his power." Under this vicious scheme, Harrison said, the government "absorbs by indirect taxes the honest wages of the labourer and doles out to him again a starving portion." The lesson of England's experience for the eighteen-year-old political economist was not the superiority of laissez-faire but instead the necessity of framing public policy so that it truly fulfilled benevolent aims.[16]

Among those in the audience on that June day at Miami was Carrie Scott. After Ben's arrival at Oxford, their relationship had matured into a firm bond, and before long, they had become engaged. But Carrie had another year of school, and the newly minted graduate was hardly prepared to support a family. Marriage would have to wait while he trained for his profession.

In the nineteenth century, most aspirants to the legal profession did not attend law school but instead "read law" with an established attorney. At his father's suggestion, Harrison sought a place in the office of an eminent Cincinnati lawyer, Bellamy Storer. A native of Maine educated at Bowdoin, Storer was a Henry Clay Whig and a former congressman with a religious enthusiasm not unlike Harrison's. He put Harrison to work copying briefs and doing other office chores, but otherwise the apprentice spent most of his time poring over huge tomes and cramming as much law into his head as he could. He considered the study tedious but necessary, and he quickly came to detest the foul air and confinement of city life in Cincinnati.[17]

Separation from Carrie compounded his misery. Later in Harrison's life, many politicians and others considered him unsympathetic and cold. His family and close friends and associates knew otherwise. Certainly his love for Carrie revealed a deeply passionate nature. After several months away from her in Cincinnati, he decided that their marriage could not wait until he had finished his legal studies. While Carrie was completing her course at her father's Oxford Female Institute, she had begun to teach piano at the school. The regular piano teacher, a relative and close friend, had fallen ill, and Carrie not only took over her teaching duties but devoted much time to nursing her as well. The strain of overwork eventually began to take its toll on her own health. Harrison convinced himself that a prolonged engagement would accelerate her decline. With a typically nineteenth-century mixture of romance and morbidity, he asked, "Shall I marry Carrie now and thus relieve her of those harassing doubts and fears which wear away her life, or shall I agree to stand aside and let her hasten to an early grave?"

The question was its own answer. Although he had no income, Ben assured Carrie's father that he could provide for her. They would live at The Point farm while he commuted to Cincinnati to finish his studies in Storer's office. Then after a quick admission to the bar, the young lawyer would be on the road to success. As he explained to a friend, his "one prevailing over-ruling characteristic" was "a determination to succeed spite of every human obstacle. . . . A 'faint heart' never did anything worthy of a man." Reverend Scott consented and married the couple in Oxford on October 20, 1853. In less than a month Caroline Harrison was pregnant.[18]

Early in 1854, the twenty-year-old Harrison won admission to the bar. He resolved to leave Cincinnati in order, as he put it, to "cut my leading strings and acquire an identity of my own." In March he scouted out Indianapolis, where he enjoyed a warm reception from Hoosiers who harbored an affectionate memory of his grandfather. He also received encouragement from his cousin William Sheets, a successful businessman and politician. Sheets talked up the city's business advantages, and, as an elder in the Presbyterian church, he also extolled its congenial spiritual atmosphere. "Most of the members of the Bar are moral, and some of them are pious men," Sheets wrote. "The standard of morality among the better class of society is very high." Ben and Carrie decided to make Indianapolis their home.[19]

In 1854 Indianapolis was still a mere town of sixteen thousand, but rapid growth had begun with the advent of railroad connections. In April the Harrisons set off for the city they would call home for the rest of their lives. Able to ship all their worldly goods in one large box for 91¢ in freight charges, the couple endured their first two years of marriage in straitened circumstances. Ben had inherited a bit of property in Cincinnati, which he sold for $800, and his father, then serving in Congress, vowed to provide another $500. They would need every cent while Harrison endeavored to begin his practice. Clients were so scarce that he gladly accepted appointment as court crier for the federal district court at $2.50 per day. After a few months, Carrie, who needed rest and medical attention, decided to complete the term of her pregnancy at her parents' home in Oxford, where, on April 12, 1854, she gave birth to a boy, Russell.[20]

Once the family was reunited, they continued to struggle financially. Service as an aide on a handful of highly visible cases won Harrison high marks for his diligence and quick mind. In his first trial, assisting the county attorney in a burglary case, he gave the summation for the prosecution. He drafted a detailed speech, but when the dim lighting at an evening court session prevented his reading it, he laid his notes aside, subdued a sense of desperation, framed a cogent and telling argument from memory, and secured a conviction. Thenceforward, careful preparation but extemporaneous presentation remained the hallmarks of his powerful public speaking.

But this triumph notwithstanding, Harrison's practice still attracted few clients or fees, and Carrie and the baby returned to Ohio for several months. "You do not know how disheartened I feel sometimes at the prospect of sitting in my office for long months without getting anything to do," he wrote her. "But however much I may be discouraged at the prospect, I never suffer myself to falter in my purpose. I have long since made up my mind that with God's blessing and good health I *would* succeed, and I never allow myself to doubt the result." Finally, after a year in Indianapolis, Harrison got his big break. In the spring of 1855, William Wallace, a successful local attorney and son of a former governor, invited the twenty-one-year-old lawyer into partnership. A candidate for the Marion County clerkship, Wallace needed someone to look after his firm's business while he campaigned. Harrison jumped at the chance. Wallace lost the election but kept Harrison on. Thanks to the senior partner's connections and the junior's intelligence and hard work, the firm of Wallace and Harrison flourished.[21]

In both bad times and good, religion remained a dominant force in Harrison's life. He and Carrie immediately joined the First Presbyterian Church when they arrived in Indianapolis. Three years later the church made Harrison a deacon. The Harrisons' social life revolved around the church, and at home prayers and Bible reading formed an important part of their daily routine. "The day of the Lord will *surely come*," Harrison penned in a private memorandum. "What manner of persons ought we to be[?] . . . We ought to live so as to *escape* the general destruc[tio]n."[22]

Harrison had not forgotten his notion that a good Christian could serve his God by taking part in politics. John Scott Harrison warned his son to steer clear of the snares of political life, but just at the time Benjamin was coming of age, the country was ablaze with the question of slavery, which infused politics with a deeply moral purpose. The Whig Party, the party of William Henry Harrison and the natural home for Benjamin and his father, had collapsed in the wake of its national defeat in 1852. The Harrisons, like thousands of others, cast about for new political fellowship, and the slavery question inevitably entered their calculation. From Congress, John Scott sent reports of the momentous fight against Stephen Douglas's Kansas-Nebraska Bill, which repealed the Missouri Compromise and opened previously free territory to slavery. John Scott threw his lot with the Know-Nothing, or American, Party, which sought to exploit a growing antipathy for immigrants as a way to deflect sectional divisiveness over the slavery question. Ben, instead, chose to align himself with the nascent Republican Party, whose cardinal principle was opposition to the spread of human bondage. In this break, he asserted his independence from his father and embraced the political identity he retained for the rest of his life.[23]

Harrison made a few stump speeches during his partner's clerk-ship campaign in 1855, but his real political initiation came the next year. As John Scott supported the American Party presidential nominee Millard Fillmore, Ben backed the Republican Party's first national candidate, John C. Frémont. When news of Frémont's nom-ination reached Indianapolis, local Republican enthusiasts gathered for a celebration and speech making. According to later stories, a deputation descended upon Harrison, who was working in his law office, and insisted that he address the crowd. He pleaded that he was unprepared, but the group insisted, carrying him out to the platform where, to add cachet to the novice's remarks, the chair-man introduced him as the grandson of William Henry Harrison. "I want it understood," the twenty-two-year-old orator began, "that I am the grandson of nobody. I believe every man should stand on his own merits." The story may be apocryphal, but it nonetheless symbolized how Harrison wrestled with the weight of his name. Although he was proud of his family heritage and benefited from the doors it opened, he rarely invoked it overtly and remained deeply conscious of a need to prove himself. "Fame is truly honorable and fortune only desirable when they have been *earned*," he had earlier written a friend. "Charity-given bread may nourish the body but it does not invigorate the soul like the hard *earned* loaf."[24]

Frémont's defeat disappointed Harrison but did not derail his own ambitions. In the spring of 1857, he won his first election, as city attorney for Indianapolis. Ambitious young lawyers like Harrison often found such a position attractive, less for its meager salary (four hundred dollars in this case) or the joy of the mostly routine work, than for the publicity it gave a fledgling lawyer and politician. The next year, he became secretary of the Republican state central committee, thereby gaining entry into the inner circle of state party leaders. His new responsibilities taught him lessons in organization and campaign management that proved valuable throughout his career. In April 1858, meanwhile, Harrison's domestic responsibilities multiplied when Carrie gave birth to their second child, Mary.

The slavery issue once again dominated the off-year election campaign of 1858. From Indianapolis, party secretary Harrison played a pivotal role in coordinating the efforts of local committees throughout the state. The results were mixed. The Democrats won the minor statewide offices contested that year but, to Harrison's delight, the Republicans won a majority in the legislature and seven of the state's eleven congressional seats.[25]

Despite his increased engagement in politics, Harrison had no desire to slight his profession. In 1860 he moved to combine the two by making a run for the position of reporter of the state supreme court. The job entailed assembling the court's opinions and publishing them in annual volumes. Proceeds from the sale of the books netted the reporter a handsome sum on top of what he could earn in his private practice. After a spirited floor fight at the state convention, Harrison won the nomination. In the general election, he faced Democrat Michael Kerr, an older, more experienced lawyer, former state representative, and future Speaker of the national House of Representatives.

On the stump that year, Harrison spent much of his time exhorting Hoosiers to vote for Abraham Lincoln. Once again, he clashed with his father, who campaigned in Ohio for the Constitutional Union ticket headed by John Bell. At one point, after a speech in which Harrison vehemently condemned the aggressions of the "slave oligarchy" and the arrogance of southerners in Washington, he received a sound rebuke from John Scott, who countered that such inflammatory rhetoric would offend "many a friend of your Grandfather." Benjamin moderated his language, but his essential message remained unchanged. In his more than eighty stump speeches, he often quoted Henry Clay's pledge that he would "never, by word or thought, by mind or will, aid in admitting to one rood of Free Territory the Everlasting Curse of Human Bondage." Harrison won his own election by a comfortable margin, and Lincoln carried the state.[26]

Harrison took office in January 1861. The reporter's position required considerable labor piled on top of the demanding load of his private practice, and he found less and less time for home and family; moreover, his church elected him, at age twenty-seven, an elder, a post he held until his death. (This attainment clearly pleased John Scott, who wrote, "He who wears worthily the honors of the Church of Christ cannot fail to be a worthy recipient of the honors of his country.") In the nation, meanwhile, the secession crisis sparked by Lincoln's election deepened. Harrison took time to listen to a speech by the president-elect on his way to Washington, and found comfort in the new leader's strength and composure. Still, when war came at Fort Sumter in April, Harrison resisted the impulse to emulate his military grandfather and did not answer Lincoln's first call for volunteers. He was already performing public service as court reporter, Carrie was pregnant with their third child, and a brother and nephew were living under his roof and dependent upon his income. In June the baby, a girl, died at birth, and this first great sorrow in the Harrisons' married life made it even less likely that Ben would soon leave Carrie to enlist in what many believed would be a short fight.[27]

As the war ground on, however, the prospect of a quick Union victory dimmed. In July 1862 Lincoln requisitioned the states to furnish an additional three hundred thousand troops, and Indiana governor Oliver P. Morton was disappointed at the slow pace of Hoosier enlistments. In a meeting with Harrison, the governor expressed his discouragement that men were engaging in mundane private pursuits while the rebellion threatened to destroy the country. Harrison immediately offered his services, and Morton responded that he would be pleased to have him lend a hand with recruitment. But Harrison was unwilling to ask other men to do something he would not do himself. He agreed not only to recruit but to enlist, whereupon Morton commissioned him a second lieutenant. He left immediately, and, as a friend later wrote, the new officer "bought a military cap . . . engaged a fifer and drummer, returned to his office, threw a flag out of the window, and began recruiting." Within a month the Seventieth Indiana Volunteer Regiment was filled, and Benjamin Harrison was its colonel. He entrusted his legal business to his partner and selected a deputy to conduct his reporter's business. With his family's financial support thus assured, he was ready to fight to save the Union.

Like most northern soldiers, Harrison saw a moral dimension in that fight, but more than most, he viewed the crusade through the lens of his personal religious commitment. As he took the field, he wrote Carrie to pray to God "1st That he will enable me to bear myself as a good soldier of Jesus Christ. 2 That he will give me valor and skill to conduct myself so as to honor my country and my friends and *lastly* that if consistent with his holy will, I may be brought 'home again' to the dear loved ones."[28]

Harrison had no illusions that he had somehow inherited military talent from his grandfather. He knew that, like his conquest of the law, success as a soldier would require study and hard work. The Seventieth performed garrison and guard duty for its first year and a half, first in Kentucky and then in Tennessee.[29] The new colonel had ample time to pore over works on warfare and to train his men. Because he had raised the regiment primarily in Indianapolis and its environs, many of its members knew each other, and most had heard of Harrison as a prominent lawyer and officeholder. This familiarity compounded the difficulty of inducing men to exchange the easygoing ways of peace for military discipline.

Even so, Harrison's temperament was, in one sense at least, well suited to the task, for he had always tried to live an orderly, rule-driven life. Knowing that his slight physical stature commanded no deference, he moved quickly to establish the respect owed to his rank. He enacted strict discipline, banning liquor from camp and drilling incessantly. Some men found his authority oppressive and even complained in letters to their hometown newspapers, but Harrison was determined to whip his thousand greenhorns into an efficient fighting force. "I am glad to know," he wrote Carrie, "that my men have confidence in me when a fight is talked of, however much they may *grumble* about the strictness of my discipline."[30]

Harrison described one of the grumblers as "a blatant infidel [who] hates me for the religious influence I attempt to exert in the reg[imen]t." The born-again colonel made no excuses for his Christian convictions. He held religious services and "family prayers" in camp, tried to enforce some semblance of repose on the Sabbath, read religious tracts to men in the camp hospital, and otherwise sought to promote a "sense of Christian patriotism." After eight months, he took satisfaction that God's grace had made some progress, "even in bring[ing] some sinners to a knowledge of himself."[31]

One of the sins that irked Harrison most was drunkenness, among officers as well as enlisted men. And yet, despite his fastidiousness and reserve, the compulsory camaraderie with his fellow officers forced him to lose some of his social stiffness and isolation. He attended parties and dinners where he enjoyed sipping just enough wine "to give vivacity to the mind." He admitted to Carrie that his ability to make a speech and drink a toast surprised many of his brother officers who "from my quiet reserve at table have probably voted me a *bore*." He never went in for dancing, backslapping, or swapping vulgar stories, but life in the army wrought some mellowing of Harrison's social persona.[32]

The Seventieth Indiana, as part of the Army of the Cumberland, finally joined the hot war in the Atlanta Campaign led by Union general William T. Sherman. As Harrison prepared for battle, he wrote Carrie that if he should die, "let your grief be tempered by the consolation that I died for my Country & in Christ." In the first major fighting of the campaign at Resaca, Harrison led a frontal assault and captured a well-defended Confederate battery, netting a haul of four large guns and twelve hundred small arms. After this fight, the Indiana colonel was put in command of a brigade that included four regiments in addition to the Seventieth. He remained a brigade commander until the end of the war. Harrison's leadership at Resaca won high praise from his father and in the newspapers back home. With understandable pride, he wrote Carrie that he had shown that the family's "famous name is as safe in my keeping as in that of any who now bear the name. We must not however think too much of the praises of the newspapers, nor forget that to God who sustains me belongs all the honor."[33]

As Sherman pressed on toward Atlanta during the summer of 1864, Harrison and his men came in for hard fighting. Indeed, as several of his biographers have noted, Harrison took part in more battles in a month than William Henry Harrison had fought in his life. His early study and strict training paid off, for his regiment remained disciplined and effective. After one particularly bloody engagement, when his regiment became separated from its surgeons, the colonel rolled up his sleeves to dress men's wounds himself. Like many other officers in the war, Harrison discovered, perhaps with some surprise, that he had the capacity to lead men, even into extreme peril. "I have got to love them for their bravery and for dangers we have shared together," he wrote Carrie. "I have heard similar expressions from the men towards me." One young lieutenant who crossed Harrison complained that he tended to "treat his inferiors like dogs," but that seems to have been a minority opinion.[34]

In any event, Harrison won the notice of his superiors. After he showed particular valor in the Union defeat of a Confederate attack at Peach Tree Creek, General "Fighting Joe" Hooker promised, "Harrison, by G-d, I'll make you a Brigadier Genl for this fight." Harrison was gratified by the confidence but was a bit leery of rising too rapidly beyond his experience or his deserts, which he thought had been "the ruin of more than one good officer." "I should like to wear the 'lone star,' when I can feel that I have *won* it," he wrote Carrie on his thirty-first birthday, "but my own ambition does not soar very high. . . . I am not a Julius Ceasar [*sic*] nor a Napoleon, but a plain Hoosier Colonel, with no more relish for a fight than for a good breakfast & *hardly* so much." Despite Hooker's warm recommendation to Secretary of War Edwin Stanton, Harrison did not receive his appointment as a brevet brigadier general until near the war's end.[35]

Atlanta fell to Sherman in early September 1864, and ten days later Harrison headed home under orders to report to Governor Morton for "special duty." That duty included recruitment of new soldiers and, more important, campaigning for the Republican ticket in the fall elections. After Harrison had entered the army in 1862, Hoosier Democrats had secured a court order declaring the supreme court reporter's office vacant, and in a special election, Democrat Michael Kerr had defeated an ineffectual Republican candidate. In 1864 the Republicans nominated Harrison again for the position. He stumped the state vigorously, adjuring voters to stand by the Republicans and the war effort and accusing the Democrats of halfhearted resistance to, if not outright sympathy for, the rebellion. He condemned the Democrats' notions of state sovereignty as "a deadly poison to national life." Moreover, defying the widespread negrophobia in the state, Harrison fervently defended the Emancipation Proclamation and extolled the courageous service of blacks in the effort to suppress the rebellion. Harrison and the entire state ticket triumphed, and Lincoln carried Indiana.[36]

Immediately after the election, Harrison headed for Georgia to rejoin his men. On the way, however, he received orders to take command of a brigade forming in Tennessee as part of an effort to block a Confederate counteroffensive. The brigade was a mongrel outfit with many men Harrison considered "quite unfit for duty in the field"—some hardly recovered from wounds, others just back from sick leave, and a large number of raw recruits, including many European immigrants unable to speak English. Harrison rallied the unit to some semblance of fighting shape, but it saw little real action in the defense of Nashville. Meanwhile, Harrison's regiment, the Seventieth Indiana, marched with Sherman to the sea.[37]

Harrison's return to his old command was further delayed by a bout of scarlet fever while he was on furlough, during which he received news of his brevet appointment as brigadier. He returned to the field in the Carolinas in March 1865, but temporary assignments kept him from his men until after Appomattox in April. He finally reached his brigade headquarters at Raleigh, only to learn that Lincoln had been assassinated. It was a bitter cup to come at the end, but Harrison's days as a warrior were at last done.[38]

Like many another Civil War soldier, Harrison tried to assure his wife that duty in the field had not weaned him of home. Rather, he insisted, should his life be spared, he would do all in his power to be a better husband and father. These protestations intensified as the end of the war drew near. Never again, he promised, would he make himself "a slave to my business." He could easily win election to Congress, he wrote Carrie on the eve of the Grand Review of Union troops in Washington, but he would refuse the chance. "If my ambition is to soar any more after I come home, you will have to give it wings, for I certainly long only for a life of quiet usefulness at Home."[39]

# 2

---

# The Path to "Future Fruit"

At Golgotha Church in Georgia in 1864, Colonel Benjamin Harrison and his men stood "fighting an unseen enemy for an hour & ½ without flinching," even though, the colonel wrote, some "men had their heads torn off close down to the shoulders." Such scenes of horror and sacrifice cut indelible gashes in the psyche of Harrison and countless other Civil War soldiers. Little wonder, then, that he and other northerners were determined to ensure that at the war's end such carnage had bought not merely a surcease from fighting but a true and lasting peace. Southern rebels, they believed, should willingly accept the new political and social order that emancipation and defeat had wrought.

Nonetheless, as the drama of Reconstruction unfolded and southern intransigence persisted, the futility of such northern hopes became clear. White southern conservatives were determined to salvage as much of their old order as possible. As early as August 1865, Harrison warned an audience of returning soldiers in Indianapolis that their southern foes were "just as wily, mean, impudent, and devilish as they ever were. . . . Beaten by the sword, they will now fall back on 'the resources of statesmanship.'" Politics would be the new battleground where ex-rebels, and their sympathizers in the northern Democratic Party, would strive to undo what Lincoln, Grant, and Sherman, as well as Harrison and the Hoosier boys in blue, had accomplished. Harrison did not advocate immediate enfranchisement of the former slaves, but if white southerners remained recalcitrant, he thought that the adoption of black suffrage offered the only way to produce truly loyal governments in the South. The key to a successful peace was to keep the rebels and "their Northern allies out of power. If you don't," Harrison warned, "they will steal away, in the halls of Congress, the fruits won from them at the glistening point of the bayonet." To prevent that loss of the peace became the cardinal purpose of Harrison and most other Republicans in the immediate postwar years.[1]

Despite pleas that he run for Congress, Harrison confined his own political efforts in this period to stump speaking. He had not abandoned ambition altogether, but he was now focused on laying a sound financial footing for himself and his family. He labored feverishly in his job as supreme court reporter and in his private practice, and by 1867, his annual income exceeded $10,000 (more than $120,000 in today's dollars). But the hard work exacted a toll, and in the spring of that year exhaustion drove him to the point of collapse. He learned his lesson. While he recovered, he concluded that he could forgo running for another term as court reporter. And he took an extended hunting and fishing trip in Minnesota, the first of many such excursions as he sought a more healthful balance of work and rejuvenation.[2]

In short order, Harrison moved to the front rank of the Indiana bar. Moreover, in his litigation with political dimensions he excelled as an exponent of Republican Party doctrine in the courtroom as much as on the stump. One such courtroom battle involved a suit growing out of the famous Civil War treason trials in Indiana. In 1864 a military commission convicted Lambdin P. Milligan and several other Democratic opponents of the war for engaging in allegedly treasonable activity. Two years later, the U.S. Supreme Court, in the landmark case *Ex Parte Milligan*, overturned the convictions on the grounds that military commissions were illegal when civilian courts were functioning. Subsequently, Milligan sought damages from the commission members and other officials, and President Ulysses S. Grant asked Harrison to represent them.

In the suit, argued in 1871, Harrison offered an impassioned defense of the military commissioners for doing their duty under orders at a time of grave peril. Milligan and other southern sympathizers in the North had, he said, "protracted the war" by "holding out aid and comfort to the enemy." Delivered against the backdrop of the guerrilla warfare that the Ku Klux Klan and similar groups were waging against the Republican state governments in the South, Harrison's argument left scant room to doubt that the Democratic Party could not yet be trusted to preserve the results of the war. Milligan won the suit on the points of law, but the damage award of five dollars lent sanction to Harrison's contentions. The *Indianapolis Journal*, the state Republican organ, hailed him as a lawyer with "no superior at the bar of Indiana" and "the ablest public speaker of the State."[3]

The next year, 1872, seemed propitious for Harrison to return to the political arena, and he threw his hat in the ring for the Republican nomination for governor. In a crowded field of candidates, he quickly rose to the upper tier, and many considered him the odds-on favorite. Yet no one could expect to prevail without the approval of the state party leader, former governor Oliver P. Morton. Hoosier Republicans revered Morton for his intrepid leadership during the war. In 1867 they had rewarded him with a seat in the U.S. Senate. With easy access to patronage favors from his friend President Grant, Morton held a firm grip on the party's organization. In the selection of nominees to run for state offices, he preferred compliant allies over potential rivals. On the eve of the state convention in 1872, murmurs circulated through the hotel crowds that Harrison was "a stinking little aristocrat" as well as cool toward Morton. Whether or not the senator inspired the grumbling, Harrison himself compounded the irritation by refusing to mingle in the lobbies to cultivate support. The next day, by a two-to-one margin, the del-

egates nominated Thomas M. Browne, a lesser-known and somewhat bibulous friend of the senator. But Harrison served himself
well in a gracious concession speech that struck a keynote for the
campaign. The Republicans' mission "to bring freedom and equal
rights to the enslaved of the land" would not end, he told the delegates, "until civil affairs have been settled on an enduring basis of
justice in the Southern States . . . and until the humble cabin of the
negro is made safe against the midnight assaults of barbarion [sic]
Democrats."[4]

Though out of office, Harrison could console himself by his continued success at the law. The Panic of 1873 and the ensuing and prolonged depression made little dent in his own prosperity. Indeed,
the explosion of bankruptcies, foreclosures, and delinquencies
swelled his firm's business. While many other citizens of Indianapolis scraped along, he and Caroline superintended the construction
of a new house on fashionable North Delaware Street in 1874 and
1875. Costing more than twenty-one thousand dollars to build, the
massive brick home was far roomier than the cramped quarters the
family would later find upstairs at the White House. The Harrisons
settled into a comfortable life, Carrie managing the household, pursuing her interest in painting, and performing the duties of a society
matron.[5]

Yet, despite his success, Harrison never acquired a sense of entitlement or, indeed, of true financial security. Years later he wrote a
friend, "Though I have worked hard all my life and made a good
deal of money, there has always been some present demand for
most of it." Even in his postpresidential years, he remained dependent upon the practice of law.[6]

If the depression of the 1870s did not threaten Harrison's personal finances, it played havoc with the government's fiscal and
monetary affairs, and thereby altered the political landscape. Republicans, who had put Grant in the White House in 1868 and again in
1872 and had dominated the national government for more than a

decade, would now have to run against hard times. Issues related to the South and civil rights shared attention with economic concerns, particularly the so-called money question.

During the Civil War, the federal government, hard up for cash, had issued some four hundred million dollars in greenbacks, Treasury notes unbacked by specie. What to do with this fiat money formed a central issue in the postwar decades. Those who supported hard money, either as a matter of sound principle or as creditors hoping to profit from deflation, favored retiring the greenbacks or backing them with gold as soon as feasible. Soft money advocates, especially debtors looking to ease their burdens, favored retaining or even expanding the greenbacks and were less fastidious about the speedy resumption of specie payments. The Panic put the issue at center stage, but it cut across political party lines. Easterners tended to favor hard money, while those from the West and South inclined toward soft money. The inability of either the Republicans or the Democrats to present a united front gave rise to several third parties that called for inflation.[7]

Indiana proved a fertile breeding ground for greenbackism. In Congress Morton took the lead in the spring of 1874 in favor of legislation to pump forty-four million dollars in retired greenbacks back into the economy. Grant's veto of this so-called Inflation Bill stunned the Indiana senator and other Republican inflationists. Harrison, however, embraced the president's action. Although he touted the greenbacks as "the best currency this country ever saw," he perceived no need to expand it. Indeed, he told a campaign audience that fall, "It is better to have a little less currency than we need than it would be to have more; for whenever we have an excess, speculation is stimulated to an excessive degree, and the currency becomes depreciated." At its root, he believed, the issue had a moral dimension. "There is in this country," Harrison said, "perhaps, too much haste to be rich. We have almost forgotten the old, slow way, and can hardly be content with a fortune that it takes a life time of honest toil to accumulate. Men who are poor to-day think they must put on to-morrow the equipage and style of wealth. This is all wrong, and an admonition such as we had [in the Panic] last fall was a good thing for us."

This seems an odd bit of political rhetoric at a time when depression cast its shadow across the land. But in this same year, Mark Twain and Charles Dudley Warner's best-selling novel, *The Gilded Age*, savagely satirized greedy speculators and political corruption. Like many Americans, Harrison saw the Panic as the inevitable consequence of years of feverish speculation whose promise of quick riches had lured too many people from old republican notions of steady labor and virtuous habits. The remark also reflected Harrison's sense of his own life course, which taught that hard work was the key to success. An indispensable concomitant to that maxim, however, was the ideal of equal and unfettered opportunity—that the road to success should be open to all strivers. Nowhere was that ideal more defiled than in the South, still plagued by racial violence. "That land is full of blood," Harrison told Hoosier voters. "Who can doubt that these rivers of blood which the Southern earth has drunk since the war closed call with a mighty voice for the condemnation of the world and the vengeance of God?"[8]

Still, Harrison's attitude on the money question did not discourage opponents bent on sniffing out any whiff of the "stinking aristocrat." In early 1876 they thought they found further evidence in a politically charged legal case involving the Whiskey Ring, a far-flung conspiracy to defraud the federal government of excise taxes. Harrison headed the defense for Hiram Brownlee, an internal revenue officer and a scion of a prominent Republican family, who was accused of taking a five-hundred-dollar bribe from distiller John Bingham. Having turned state's evidence, Bingham swore he gave Brownlee the money, and a canceled check supported his assertion. But in a brilliant diversionary tactic, Harrison zeroed in on Bingham's observation that at the handover, Brownlee, about to serve as a groomsman in a wedding, was wearing white kid gloves. When another groomsman swore that Brownlee arrived at the wedding without gloves, Harrison skillfully exploited the discrepancy to discredit Bingham's entire testimony. The ploy worked. The jury returned a verdict of not guilty and Harrison came away with added renown as a brilliant lawyer, though Democrats cast him as a clever paladin of the kid-gloves set.[9]

As the 1876 nominating season approached, Harrison again attracted support for governor, and some Republicans even began to tout the forty-two-year-old lawyer as a candidate for the presidency. The latter notion was at best wildly premature, though John Scott Harrison was confident that such "complimentary notices" of his son would "bring future fruit." As for the governorship, both father and son concluded that Harrison's continued uneasy relationship with Morton argued against his making another run for the nomination.[10]

But fate had another idea. In August a conflict-of-interest scandal forced the withdrawal of the Republicans' gubernatorial nominee, and desperate party leaders needed a replacement who could grasp the situation and launch an aggressive campaign. They turned to Harrison, and he accepted. His Democratic opponent, James D. Williams, was a rural congressman who affected a rustic image in his trademark homespun suit, and the Democrats cast the race as one of "Blue Jeans" against "Kid Gloves." The major parties were nearly equal in strength in Indiana, and the presence of a Greenback Party ticket in the race complicated the calculations of both.[11]

Within two weeks, Harrison was on the stump. On the money question, he argued that an unstable currency was most damaging to the laboring classes and the poor. Thanks to the Republican-sponsored Specie Resumption Act, the greenbacks were appreciating in value as the date—1879—approached when the Treasury would exchange them for coin. Hoping to stanch defections from the party on the question, Harrison insisted that the greenback was "a Republican boy; born in our house, bone of our bone, and flesh of our flesh." Neither the inflationist Democrats nor the Greenbackers could be trusted to rear it to parity with gold; only the Republicans could "make it stable and unchangeable in value."

At the same time, Harrison continued to emphasize the southern question. The issue was not merely the Democrats' flirtation with treason in the war; it was also the current and persistent crushing of blacks' aspirations in the South. The Democrats' takeover of the national House of Representatives two years earlier had made it impossible for the Republicans to add new protective legislation for the former slaves. Harrison insisted that the nation must not abandon them. "We entered into an obligation solemn as a covenant with our God to save these people from the dastardly outrages that their rebel masters are committing upon them in the South." When violence threatened again in South Carolina, Harrison hailed Grant's dispatch of troops to the state.[12]

Harrison lost to Williams by a margin of 1.1 percent. Immediately after the October balloting, the Republican national committee sent him off on a speaking tour through several states on behalf of presidential nominee Rutherford B. Hayes. He did not disappoint. "While speaking, he is all energy," said one account, "nervous and wiry, [he] gesticulates rapidly, putting a full point to each sentence with a rapid motion of clenched fists." Although he had narrowly missed the governorship, 1876 proved a pivotal year for Harrison. His gallant rescue operation in Indiana made him second only to Morton in the esteem of Hoosier Republicans, and his maiden campaign tour won the gratitude of national party leaders. He might have received a cabinet appointment from Hayes, but for Morton's opposition. With a growing base of support of his own, Harrison grew increasingly inclined to challenge the senator's domination.[13]

In July 1877 the Great Railroad Strike reached Indiana. Harrison's loss to Williams relieved him of having to deal with the conflict as governor but, even so, as a private citizen he played a leading role, exhibiting some sympathy for the strikers but none for the strike. By the mid-1870s, railroads had become not only an indispensable mode of transport but the nation's engine of modernization and industrial progress. But railroad companies also led the new corporations in the exploitation of workers, and wage cuts on several lines triggered the strike, which began in the East and spread rapidly.

The stoppage's unprecedented scope, coupled with its violence and the loss of life in Pittsburgh and other cities, convinced many that it was the beginning of a workers' revolution. For Harrison, whose legal training and experience had bred in him a reverence for the peaceful resolution of conflict, the strike seemed an assault on the blessings of law and order.

When the strike reached Indianapolis, Governor Williams responded cautiously, vowing that he would call out the militia only in the event of actual violence. The strikers remained peaceful and pledged to keep mail and passenger trains running. Nonetheless, many prominent citizens, including Harrison, considered the governor's response inadequate. Under the guise of a Committee of Public Safety, they proceeded to form ad hoc military companies, ostensibly to maintain order, although as Harrison later noted, their purpose was also to "aid in the suppression" of the strike.

Harrison believed, however, that the situation demanded more than a mere show of force. He also served on a Committee of Arbitration (though it was hardly that), which sponsored open discussion with the workers. At one meeting, Harrison accused the strikers of "putting their hands on the throat of commerce and destroying property by stopping the movement of freight." When the strike representatives started to leave, Harrison changed his tone, promising that the committee would use its influence to secure a response to their legitimate grievances. The next day, the committee issued a report that blamed the low wages on the railroads' rate wars, which drove the competing companies to charge rates so low that they could not yield enough revenue to pay their workers adequately. Once the strike and the obstruction of traffic had ceased, the committee said, "enlightened and sympathetic public opinion" should put pressure on the railroads to adjust their competitive practices and pay better wages.

By then, however, the citizens' show of force and the imminent arrival of two hundred army troops had brought the strike to an end. Afterward, when the federal courts moved to secure contempt convictions against strike leaders who violated injunctions, Harrison accepted "the *absolute* necessity of making examples of some of those who had so flagrantly defied the law." Yet he also urged the judge to free the men after they had served thirty days of their three-month sentences. Harrison's stout defense of order won the admiration of fellow citizens who shared his anxiety that the strike threatened social upheaval. On the other hand, his attempted even-handedness with the strikers left many unconvinced that he had workers' best interests at heart. His actions would dog his later political career.[14]

A few months after the strike, Oliver P. Morton died, and the way at last opened for Harrison to seize the reins of the Hoosier Republican Party. In 1878 he headed a spirited campaign in the state elections, aiming, if the Republicans won the legislature, to seek election to the U.S. Senate. On the eve of the party's state convention, where he was scheduled to give the keynote address, Harrison received the news that the body of his recently deceased father had been discovered at a Cincinnati medical school where grave robbers had deposited it. He dashed to Ohio to investigate the grisly affair and then returned to Indianapolis to offer the convention a rousing speech, interrupted repeatedly by applause and laughter. Two months later, he opened the fall campaign in Morton's hometown, symbolically assuming the fallen senator's mantle.

In the wake of the strike, evocations of class warfare echoed across the land. In his campaign Harrison urged workers to reject the teachings of financial quacks or communist demagogues and instead recognize that "capital and labor must unite in every enterprise." Any resort to lawlessness or violence in pursuit of rights would prove "absolutely fatal" to the interests of individuals and the nation as whole. The Republican Party, he insisted, was the true friend of the downtrodden. It had freed four million workers from the bondage of slavery, enacted homestead legislation, and secured an honest and stable currency, "one of the most necessary things to insure the prosperity of the poor man." He called for state legislation to mandate the prompt payment of wages, to require corporations to pay laborers before bondholders, and to protect poor debtors from losing their homes. For laborers, he endorsed "every aid which public sentiment and the law can give—without trenching upon constitutional restrictions or the rights of others."[15]

Once again, the Republicans fell short in the legislative elections. Although Harrison claimed to a friend that he was "not enough of a politician to be made unhappy by such results," he nonetheless felt gratified that he had "made some reputation by my speeches." The next year, he received a consolation prize when President Hayes appointed him to the federal Mississippi River Commission, formed to study navigation improvements and the problem of flooding on the great waterway.[16]

With Morton's passing, Harrison quickly became the acknowledged leader of the Republican Party in the key swing state of Indiana. Over the next decade, he emerged as one who not only effectively espoused the party's principles but also helped formulate its doctrine. In a speech to young Republicans in March 1880, he portrayed the party as "the party which represented the moral conscience of the people of America." At the heart of the party's creed, he maintained, was the ideal of free labor and upward mobility. "It has never placed a barrier in the way of any man who was striving for the elevation or betterment of his condition in life. It has always sympathized with and aided the efforts of every class of people who were seeking a larger liberty and a more perfect sphere for the development of their powers."[17]

Harrison headed the Indiana delegation at the 1880 Republican National Convention, where there was some talk of his being nominated for president as a dark horse, or for vice president if James G. Blaine or some other man from the East filled the top of the ticket. Harrison and most of the Indiana delegation favored Blaine, but the convention deadlocked between the Maine senator and former president Grant. More than thirty ballots ensued. Harrison, in a crucial moment, persuaded the Hoosiers to switch to James A. Garfield, who was present as an Ohio delegate and who took the nomination on the next ballot. On an early ballot, Harrison had received one vote, and he now used this fact to good advantage in a call to make Garfield's nomination unanimous. He drew hearty laughter from the delegates when he said that even though he was "the only defeated candidate for the Presidency on the floor of this Convention," he bore Garfield "no malice." "I will defer my speech until the campaign is hot," he declared, "and then, on every stump in Indiana, and wherever else my voice can help this great Republican cause on to victory, I hope to be found."[18]

He kept his promise. He stumped Indiana and then headed to other states, including New York, where vice presidential nominee Chester Arthur pleaded, "We need General Harrison." The return of good economic times proved a potent ally to the Republicans. Garfield won and the party carried a majority of seats in the Indiana legislature. Harrison then signaled his intention to run for the U.S. Senate. Although Garfield would have been happy to have him in his cabinet, Harrison preferred the Senate seat, which would leave him time enough to continue his legal practice.[19]

Harrison's only serious opponent for the Senate was Walter Q. Gresham, who had been federal district judge for Indiana since 1869. The two men had occasionally tangled in court and had little love for each other in their rivalry for the party's leadership after Morton's death. Gresham had a reform image and a warmer personality than Harrison's and was well connected with national party leaders. But his position on the bench prevented him from stump speaking or performing the other public party duties at which Harrison excelled. After a few weeks, Gresham withdrew, and Harrison sailed to an easy victory when the legislature voted. Harrison would go to Washington, but he and Gresham would clash again.[20]

Harrison served six years in the Senate, too short a time for him to move into the front rank of senators occupied by such men as John Sherman of Ohio. Still, he won plaudits as a competent legislator and party spokesman, despite his surprise at the work load. "Life here is slavish to those who feel like conscientiously trying to do their duty," he wrote a friend early in his term. "You know I used to be a hard worker at home, but . . . [h]ere I have no time *out of bed* that is my own." Living in relatively small quarters in Washington, he and Carrie held a few receptions, but Harrison did not travel in the inner circle of the Senate club. During his last session, Carrie stayed in Indianapolis, and the lonesome senator found that the "evenings sometimes hang very heavily. I could find company no doubt but I am not a good hand at doing it."[21]

Early in his term, Harrison spent much of his time fielding patronage requests from office-hungry Hoosiers. This helped him solidify his following at home, but it was onerous, often unappreciated labor. Some relief from the patronage burden came with the passage of the Pendleton Civil Service Act. He supported the reform measures, although he argued strongly, and successfully, for allowing federal employees to make voluntary monetary contributions to their party.[22]

Much of his work, however, encompassed the crafting and negotiation of legislation. One of the principal problems confronting the nation in Harrison's time was the federal government's collection of an excess revenue, which withdrew money from the private economy. During the Civil War, Congress had greatly increased import tariffs and internal duties to meet military expenses. Although taxes had been lowered somewhat after the war, every year since 1866 the government had collected a surplus of revenue, often far beyond current expenditures. Democrats, true to the long-standing doctrine of their southern wing, favored cutting the tariff to reduce the revenue. Republicans opposed any deep cuts that would jeopardize the protection of American producers from foreign competition. The issue had played an important part in the 1880 election, and now, as a senator, Harrison defended protectionism. Although he would accept the reduction of some rates, he was much more willing to reduce the revenue through the elimination of internal duties on nearly all commodities except alcohol and tobacco.

In addition, from a political standpoint, defending tariff protectionism offered a way for Harrison to offset his "kid-gloves" image and ally himself with American labor. A tariff for revenue only, which the Democrats advocated, "means less work and lower wages," he argued. "I do not say that labor has its full reward here. I do not deny that the avarice of the mill owner too often clips the edge of comfort from the wages of his operative. . . . But in spite of all this I do affirm that there is more comfort and more hope for a laboring man or woman in this country than in any other." Without the protective tariff, he insisted, that comfort and hope would be gone.[23]

Rather than jeopardize protection to reduce the surplus, Harrison thought the government could spend much of the excess revenue in beneficial ways. He particularly advocated a generous pension policy for Union veterans of the Civil War. He sponsored 101 special pension bills as well as a general bill to pension all disabled veterans, which in 1884 passed the Senate but failed in the Democratic House.[24] He supported expenditure on national public works, such as improving the navigation of the Mississippi River, although he opposed federal funding of land reclamation along the river, which he saw as the states' responsibility under the Constitution. In 1882 he voted against the annual Rivers and Harbors Bill, so notorious for local pork-barrel schemes that it drew President Arthur's veto, though in subsequent years Harrison tended to favor such bills, particularly if they included Indiana projects.[25]

Harrison also supported federal aid to education, aimed primarily at the South's illiterate population. On the Senate floor, he secured amendments that tightened pending legislation in important ways. One called for the appropriation of money on a matching basis to encourage the states themselves to increase their education spending. He made the bold step of inserting a provision that would bar funding to any state that could not certify that it provided "free common schools for all of its children of school age, without distinction of race or color." "Unless the black boy and girl in the South can share equally in the privileges of education," he declared, "then I am opposed to the bill, because it will not reach the evil that we are endeavoring to eradicate." The Senate passed the education bill several times but, again, it failed in the House.[26]

Harrison's most significant disagreement with his Republican colleagues in the Senate came in his opposition to the Chinese Exclusion Bill of 1882. As a lawyer, he argued that the bill went beyond the class of laborers whose immigration the United States could legally suspend under an 1880 treaty with China. His reasoning, of course, rested more on constitutional grounds than on sympathy for the Chinese. Constitutional scruple also governed his acquiescence in the Supreme Court's invalidation in 1883 of the Civil Rights Act of 1875, which had guaranteed equal access to public accommodations. The Court declared that the Fourteenth Amendment outlawed discrimination by states, not by individuals. The narrowness of the Court's interpretation of the amendment might require a new addition to the Constitution, Harrison told a protest meeting of blacks in Indianapolis, although he doubted "whether in the present condition of parties in this country, we could ever pass such an amendment again."[27]

The condition of parties was much on Harrison's mind as the presidential election year of 1884 approached. As the race for the Republican nomination took shape, Arthur and James G. Blaine emerged as the front-runners, but Harrison attracted—and cultivated—support as a potential alternative in the event of a convention deadlock. His strength lay in his name recognition, his service in the war, his record in the Senate, and his fine talent for expounding party doctrine on the stump, which he had gladly employed in the interest of Senate colleagues and other Republicans across the nation. Residence in Indiana—which, along with New York, was one of the most important swing states in presidential elections— boosted his chances. Harrison's supporters sought to position him as a legatee of Blaine's support, should the Maine statesman falter, and they also curried favor with the party's smaller independent, or reform, wing.

But Harrison's strategy was met by a disarmingly similar one mounted by his nemesis in Indiana, Walter Q. Gresham. In the spring of 1883, Arthur had chosen Gresham to be postmaster general, and Harrison had watched his own influence over Hoosier patronage decline. In 1884 Gresham's followers touted him as a potential heir to Arthur's nomination support, and they too wooed the party's independents, who found him more attractive than Harrison.

For either man to make a convincing showing in the national convention, he would need Indiana's backing. The spring of 1884 witnessed a fierce contest between the Harrison and Gresham camps for delegates. From the thirty Hoosier delegates, Harrison and Gresham each won a loyal core, the remainder willing to go to the man who received support from other states. Harrison decided to attend the convention as a delegate-at-large, a move that fed Gresham's apprehension that Harrison aimed to be the Garfield of a deadlocked convention—or at least was determined to prevent Gresham's nomination.

At the Chicago convention, the most important tactical question for the Harrison men was whether to have Indiana present him as a formal candidate. In the delegation's first caucus, Gresham's managers defeated such a move by a vote of sixteen to fourteen. But the next day Harrison's men returned with a nonbinding resolution for the senator's nomination, which passed, sixteen to fourteen. Harrison, believing his name was to be placed in nomination, went home to Indianapolis. Still, twelve Gresham delegates said they would not vote for the senator, and, more important, Blaine's managers complained that Harrison was keeping needed Indiana votes from the Maine leader. In the end, the Hoosiers did not present Harrison's name, the majority of them voted for Blaine, and Blaine won the nomination. Gresham's friends ridiculed Harrison's convention conduct as a "*hari kari* act in the clown's cap and bells." Even so, Harrison told his manager that after Gresham's elimination he was "glad to have you give our state an advanced standing in securing the nomination of Mr. Blaine." The Blaine men would remember the help four years later.[28]

As usual, in the fall campaign Harrison gave his help on the stump in Indiana, in Maine at Blaine's special request, and elsewhere. Moreover, when a Democratic Indianapolis newspaper published a scurrilous story that Blaine's wife had given birth to their first child three months after their marriage, the nominee tapped Harrison to launch a libel suit against the paper. Although Blaine eventually dropped the suit and lost the election to Grover Cleveland, Harrison had gathered a pocketful of chits from the Plumed Knight.[29]

Harrison's prominence continued to grow during his last two years in the Senate. As chairman of the Committee on Territories, he twice won Senate passage of a bill to admit South Dakota to the Union, but each time the majority Democrats in the House blocked statehood for the Republican-leaning territory.[30] Asserting that railroads exercised "a most dangerous and unwarranted control over the commerce of this country," Harrison supported the creation of the Interstate Commerce Commission as the best way to "re-inforce the shipper in his contest with these great railway corporations."[31] During his last session, Congress passed a version of his Dependent Pension Bill, but Cleveland blocked it as he had hundreds of individual pension bills with vetoes that Harrison described as "tipped with poisoned arrows."[32]

Besides criticizing the president for his pension parsimony, Harrison took to the Senate floor to condemn Cleveland's patronage practices. Emphasizing the issue's "humane side," the senator gave an impassioned speech in defense of one Isabelle De La Hunt, a Union veteran's impoverished widow who was eking out a living as postmistress in Cannelton, Indiana. To make way for a Democrat, Cleveland had fired Mrs. De La Hunt on the grounds of her alleged "offensive partisanship," although the administration refused to specify the charges against her. In dramatizing the "pathos and indignation" of Mrs. De La Hunt's case, Harrison debunked Cleveland's civil service pretenses, stoked Republican loyalty among old soldiers, and confirmed his bona fides with the GOP rank and file. Party committees distributed thousands of copies of the speech in Indiana and other states.[33]

The dissemination of the De La Hunt speech formed part of Harrison's campaign for reelection to the Senate. In the winter of 1885, the Democratic majority in the Indiana General Assembly had drawn the state legislative districts in a reapportionment that Harrison described as "A Bill to Prohibit the Election of a Republican United States Senator from Indiana." By May 1885, he had launched a "desperate fight" to overcome the effects of the gerrymander in the elections to choose a new legislature in the fall of 1886. From Washington he conducted a voluminous correspondence with Hoosier Republicans to ensure the selection of strong legislative candidates, even purchasing a mimeograph machine so that he could "multiply my letters." He pushed the raising and careful distribution of campaign funds, which some local party leaders intended to spend "to hold the floating vote."[34]

After Congress adjourned, Harrison took to the stump once again in Indiana. He struck familiar national themes such as tariff protection for labor and the Democrats' mismanagement of the government's finances, as well as the "disfranchisement" wrought by the gerrymander in the state. He hammered especially on Cleveland's abuse of veterans—those he had thrown out of office and those whose pensions he had blocked. In waging the hard fight, Harrison felt anxiety not only for his own success but also for the Republicans' retention of control of the Senate. The country would suffer a dark future, he believed, should it see "the last department of the general government, now held by us, pass into the hands of the Solid South and their northern allies."[35]

When the votes were counted, the Democrats wound up with a slight plurality of seats in the Indiana legislature. After a struggle of several weeks and sixteen ballots, the Democrats secured the vote of a Greenbacker and carved out a one-vote majority to elect a Democrat to replace Harrison in the Senate. But in the November election, the Republican state ticket had won handily, the GOP had taken seven of thirteen congressional seats, and, most revealing of the gerrymander's impact, in the aggregate tally for legislative candidates the Republicans had garnered some ten thousand more votes than the Democrats. In the end, Harrison scored a triumph in defeat. Having conducted so "magnificent a fight," wrote Senate colleague Preston Plumb of Kansas, "puts you in the line of Presidential promotion."[36]

# 3

## Hoosier in Command

It is impossible to know precisely when Benjamin Harrison began seriously to consider the notion that he could follow in his grandfather's footsteps to the White House. After he had won the prize, he told a friend that "the thought had been with him many times when suggested by others, but he had never been possessed by it or had his life shaped by it." Over the years, friendly newspapers and political associates had occasionally raised the idea, which he graciously acknowledged but gently pooh-poohed. To friends, he explained that his 1884 quasi candidacy had been designed primarily to thwart that of his Hoosier rival, Walter Q. Gresham. With no apparent sense of irony, he thereby confessed to a motive hardly more admirable than overweening ambition. During the 1886 campaign, Harrison had confided to close friends that he would "shed no tears" if he lost his Senate seat and that he "would greatly enjoy the opportunity to attend to my own business and let politics alone." Yet he knew that national party leaders had watched his campaign closely, and afterward he wrote a friend, "I have come out of it with more friends & reputation than ever before."[1]

In the ensuing months, moreover, he missed few opportunities to enhance that reputation. During his last session in the Senate, he accepted several invitations to address Republican gatherings where he received warm praise for his gallant reelection fight. "Though an expiring statesman," he declared in Baltimore, "I am a rejuvenated Republican. In returning again to the profession I love, . . . I do not mean to quit the politics into which I was born." To the young Republicans of Providence he promised that in 1888 Indiana would "join hands with Rhode Island and the other Republican states in electing a Republican president." He did not, of course, say that the nominee ought to come from Indiana. But after the GOP lost the 1887 state elections in the other major swing state of New York, a Buffalo Republican told Harrison what he already knew: party leaders recognized *the great importance* of Indiana and are asking 'who can carry that state?' "[2]

Such leaders and their lieutenants wielded great influence in the nineteenth century. The parties chose national convention delegates not in primary elections but in state and district conventions. In the run-up to these gatherings, newspapers boomed favorite candidates, and their backers engaged in extensive letter-writing campaigns and face-to-face persuasion to garner support. When party cadres surveyed the field of potential presidential nominees, they weighed a number of considerations: a candidate's record in public office, service in the Union army (especially important to the Republicans), fidelity to the party and its principles, ability to articulate the party's position on issues, relative freedom from factional animosities, and good standing in the doubtful states or, better yet, residence in one of them. Although Harrison's sojourn on the national political scene had been relatively short, his reputation was solid. More essential, he scored high marks on all these criteria.

As the preconvention season approached in late 1887, the odds-on Republican favorite was the 1884 nominee, James G. Blaine. In December President Cleveland devoted his entire annual message to a fervent call for tariff cuts to reduce the surplus, thus ensuring that the tariff question would take center stage in the 1888 campaign. Blaine, traveling in Europe, led the GOP response in a widely published interview that presented a spirited defense of protectionism. Blaine had thrust himself into the lead for the GOP nomination. But in fact he had no stomach for a "scramble" for delegates, and in early 1888 he announced that his name would not be presented to the national convention in Chicago. Although his statement seemed to allow for a draft and some of his supporters continued to work quietly toward that end, the friends of rival candidates took him at his word, and a fight for the nomination was on.[3]

The new front-runner was John Sherman, longtime Ohio senator and former Treasury secretary. Sherman enjoyed wide respect for his grasp of issues, especially financial questions, but his undoubted abilities did not fully compensate for an icy personality. Gresham, now a federal circuit judge in Chicago, was also in the race. His defense of railroad strikers made him popular with labor, but his tendency to favor tariff reduction cost him support among increasingly protectionist Republicans. Iowa senator William B. Allison had a reputation as a skillful legislator and party conciliator, but he sparked little popular enthusiasm. Wealthy businessmen Russell Alger of Michigan and Chauncey Depew of New York had hardly more chance than several other states' more obscure favorite sons. One thing was clear: With Blaine out of the race, his loyalists would wield great influence in selecting his successor.

No one understood this better than Benjamin Harrison. Nearly a year before the convention, Blaine lieutenant Stephen B. Elkins had told Harrison that he was a likely heir to the Plumed Knight's support. Unwilling to offend his potential benefactor, Harrison had kept a low profile before Blaine's withdrawal, telling one supporter who offered to give him a public endorsement, "I will not in any way promote any movement to make me a Presidential candidate." Meanwhile, however, a small committee headed by his chief political adviser, Louis T. Michener, was hard at work doing just that.

The day after Blaine's letter appeared, the *Indianapolis Journal* began to boom the ex-senator's candidacy. Harrison himself handsomely saluted the Maine statesman's devotion to Republican principles and told reporters that he had no doubt that Blaine had given his declination "sincerely." When Elkins wrote that the convention

might still turn to Blaine, Harrison frankly replied that the withdrawal letter would then "prove to have been a great mistake," for
disappointed rivals would resent Blaine's seeming uncandor.[4]

In the spring Harrison gave a few well-received speeches that
signaled his availability as "a living and rejuvenated Republican." He
stressed the centrality of the southern question—the continued
denial of the black vote and the consequent impact on federal policy. The right to vote, Harrison insisted, "is the dominant question at
the foundation of our Government, in its dominating influence
embracing all others, because it involves the question of a free and
fair tribunal to which every question shall be submitted for arbitra-
ment and final determination." The dependent pension bill, he
argued, "would pass over the President's veto if these black friends
of the Union soldier had their fair representation in Congress." Similarly, "the paralyzing shadow of free trade falls upon the manufactures and upon the homes of our laboring classes . . . because the
laboring vote in the Southern States is suppressed." On the tariff
issue, he declared, the Republican party "is pledged and ought to be
pledged to the doctrine of the protection of American industries
and American labor." Tariff reduction, as proposed by Cleveland,
would "interrupt this march of prosperity."[5]

After he pulled out of the race, Blaine wrote Elkins that for
"many reasons" he thought Harrison could "make the best run." But
for Harrison's candidacy to attain national viability, he needed to
demonstrate that Indiana Republicans backed him solidly. Gresham, who enjoyed the endorsement of his adopted state of Illinois,
still had many Indiana friends who had scant love for Harrison. The
Gresham crowd sought to kill off Harrison's candidacy by publiciz-
ing his Senate votes against the restriction of Chinese immigration,
a position unpopular with labor. Harrison's supporters replied
that treaty considerations had determined his votes, and they countered that Gresham's unsoundness on the tariff would endanger
protection for workers. Despite the policy debate, Harrison held a
tighter grip on the state organization and easily won endorsements
at the district and state conventions. The thirty national delegates

chosen included a handful of Gresham men, but even they agreed to vote for Harrison at least in the early rounds of balloting. After the state convention, Carrie Harrison wrote to their son, Russell, that Harrison's manager, Michener, was "laughing all over" at the result.[6]

Even before the selection of the Indiana delegates, Michener and his team had begun courting support elsewhere. They supplied delegates with issues of the *Indianapolis Journal* and other campaign information, and in May Michener traveled through the East wooing party leaders. The Harrison men did not aggressively seek converts among delegates from other candidates' home states. Instead, recognizing that a crowded field would probably lead to prolonged convention balloting, they cultivated second-choice support. Always in the forefront of their calculations was the latent Blaine sentiment. "We think we have the right to make some modest claims upon the friends of Mr. Blaine," Michener wrote Elkins, especially after "the very material support given to Mr. Blaine at a critical juncture in the last National Convention."[7]

Elkins continued to encourage Harrison and the Hoosiers, but he also kept alive the possibility of a Blaine nomination. In this, he was not alone, for a Blaine draft remained a fond hope of many eastern leaders, including New Yorkers Whitelaw Reid and Thomas C. Platt. But in late May Blaine sent Reid another, more forceful withdrawal, stating that he could "not accept" a nomination. Harrison's men saw the move as another boost for their candidate, although they would soon discover that the Blaine specter yet endured.[8]

In the first week of June 1888, the Democrats renominated Grover Cleveland on a platform calling for tariff reduction. Two weeks later, the Republican hosts gathered in Chicago, which John Hay described as "a hot and sizzling cauldron of intrigue and anxiety." Michener and his committee spearheaded Harrison's convention effort, aided by some ten thousand Hoosiers who, Michener later wrote, "thronged the hotels and lodging houses and earnestly, intelligently and persistently presented the arguments" for Harrison.

Harrison's friend and *Indianapolis Journal* editor Elijah W. Halford safeguarded the candidate's views as a member of the resolutions committee. Under the chairmanship of Ohio congressman William McKinley, a vigorous champion of protectionism, the committee produced—and the convention adopted—a platform that declared the party to be uncompromisingly in favor of the American system of protection, whose destruction as proposed by Cleveland and the Democrats would injure business, labor, and farmers. To cut the surplus, the Republicans favored eliminating internal taxes and were willing to raise some tariff rates to prohibitive levels in order to curb imports and thus check the collection of revenue. For the revenue that remained, Republicans saw a myriad of uses, including defense, veterans' pensions, internal improvements, and subsidies for the nation's ailing merchant marine. On the southern question, the platform demanded "effective legislation to secure the integrity and purity of elections." Whatever influence Halford had in writing the platform, Harrison pronounced it "clear and emphatic" and "in harmony with my views."[9]

Speakers on Thursday, June 21, placed eight candidates in nomination, but the man who appeared to have the largest potential support went unnamed. When Harrison's son-in-law, Robert McKee, arrived in Chicago, he found that, despite his two withdrawals, "Blaine is still the favorite of just lots and lots of people." The Blaine men hoped for a deadlocked convention that would turn to the old standard-bearer with near unanimity—making him an offer he could not refuse. The first ballot on Friday showed a wide dispersal of votes, which augured well for the Blaine strategy. Of fourteen men receiving votes, Sherman led with 229, barely half the number needed to win. Harrison garnered 85 votes for fourth place behind Gresham and Depew. In addition to 29 votes from Indiana (the other Hoosier vote going to Gresham), Harrison received handfuls of votes from nineteen states and two territories. Two more ballots brought little change. During a recess, Depew withdrew.

Amid the confusion, the implicit strategy of the Blaine men was to divide their votes among other candidates, testing each one by shifting a small number of votes behind one or more of them in succession to sound out their strength, demonstrate their unpopularity, and eliminate them from consideration. The first "beneficiary" of this strategy was Harrison, whose nomination was acceptable even if the strategy failed. New York, under the direction of Thomas C. Platt, was prepared to give the Hoosier five-sixths of its vote when the delegates reconvened on Friday evening, but supporters of other candidates blocked any further balloting that day. That many of the Blaine men supported this adjournment suggests that they were content to head off a Harrison stampede.[10]

On the fourth ballot, on Saturday morning, Harrison climbed to 216 votes, only 19 behind John Sherman. His votes came from two-thirds of the states, including 58 of New York's 72 votes and 20 from Wisconsin. On the next ballot, however, his total declined slightly, and, as Blaine's son Walker noted, "Everybody thought Harrison beaten and everyone believed that father would be nominated that afternoon." Ohio's Mark Hanna wired Sherman that the New York vote for Harrison was "only a cover," and after the convention recessed, Depew predicted that Blaine would be nominated by acclamation when it resumed at four o'clock. When the delegates reconvened, however, the anti-Blaine and anti-Harrison majority forced another adjournment to Monday, June 25.[11]

The weekend recess witnessed intense machinations. Deadlock continued to be the key for the Blaine men, who sought to keep Sherman in the field in order to neutralize his large, but not growing, bloc of votes. Sherman himself fairly begged that "New York do for me what she did for Indiana," and he received intimations that the Empire State would abandon Harrison and swing to him after the sixth and seventh ballots on Monday.

Tasting victory, Michener and his team circulated among the delegates, pointing out that Harrison's strength came primarily from swing states, precisely the ones needed to win against President Cleveland in November. They pleaded with the New Yorkers to stand by Harrison, promising an increase in his vote on Monday. In these efforts, Platt received the impression, whether intended or not, that he could become secretary of the Treasury in a Harrison administration. Most persuasive, however, was the arrival of Blaine's unequivocal refusal of a nomination, at last killing the maneuvers for a draft. With the solid vote of New York and the perceptible shift of Blaine's support from other states, Harrison moved ahead of Sherman on the seventh ballot on Monday. He won the nomination on the next roll call with 544 votes. Later in the day, the convention nominated New Yorker Levi P. Morton for vice president.[12]

Harrison had followed the proceedings carefully, huddled with friends around the telegraph ticker at his law office. At last the message arrived from Michener: "You are put in command." The new nominee almost fainted and had to lie down, but he soon recovered his equanimity and hurried home. There Caroline Harrison already knew the result, for hundreds of people had begun to gather on the front lawn. Soon the crowd swelled to thousands, as delegations from other cities and towns joined the citizens of Indianapolis. Before the day was over, Harrison made four short speeches from his front porch and thereby launched his election campaign.[13]

Long tradition called for a presidential nominee to discuss the issues in a formal letter of acceptance but otherwise to remain at home and leave the hard campaigning to his surrogates. In 1884 Blaine had departed from this custom—to his regret. After a grueling six-week speaking tour, he returned exhausted to New York, where in a public meeting with a group of Protestant ministers at party headquarters he failed to catch a slur one of them made against Catholics, a key constituency Blaine sought to attract. The incident may have cost him the narrow election. Harrison had no intention of duplicating Blaine's tour, but neither was the veteran campaigner content to sit quietly by. The solution was to speak to groups that came to him. "There is great risk of meeting a fool at home," he conceded, "but the candidate who travels cannot escape him."

For the nation's first front-porch campaign, the rail hub Indianapolis proved ideal to accommodate visiting delegations from around the state and country. Harrison's managers soon created a committee to impose order on these encounters with the candidate, setting the day and time for each visit. The committee required each group to appoint a chairman who would submit a short opening speech in advance to the committee, which would edit the speech before returning it for delivery. The venue for the greetings was soon changed from Harrison's front yard to the city's University Park to accommodate the large crowds. At the appointed hour, Harrison would appear, receive the greetings of the delegation, and then respond in a brief address touching upon some issue. All told, he gave over ninety speeches to more than three hundred thousand listeners. Moreover, his stenographer took down his words, and after a careful review by the nominee himself, the copy went to the Associated Press for publication nationwide in the next day's newspapers. Harrison slept in his own bed, but his message reached untold numbers of voters nearly every day.[14]

During the long struggle, Caroline Harrison stalwartly stood by her husband. She reviewed endless campaign parades, sometimes stretching for miles. On countless nights, she turned down the beds for visiting dignitaries at the Delaware Street house, and through the summer and fall, she watched a steady stream of Republicans pass by the punch bowl on her dining-room table. Daughter Mary Harrison McKee assisted her mother in campaign social duties, but the birth of Mary's second child in July limited the help she could give.

Soon after, Caroline asked her niece, Mrs. Mary Scott Dimmick, to come to Indianapolis to help with entertaining and child care. Known as Mame, Mrs. Dimmick had been a widow for six years after just three months of marriage. Thirty years old, she was four weeks younger than Mary McKee and childless. She leapt at her aunt's request, and in July found a warm welcome into the family. "Uncle Ben" particularly enjoyed her company. After a day of speeches and brass bands, when he felt that "the human voice had become *burdensome* and a quiet companion was needed," he enjoyed taking long walks with Mame, who had the good sense to talk little and give him peace. In the evening, when the family relaxed in the parlor, Ben would lie on the lounge and Mame would massage his head. In September she received an invitation to escort a younger relative on an extended trip to Europe, and she agonized about leaving the Harrisons. Aunt Carrie encouraged her to go, but "Uncle Ben said *not* to go." In the end, she left in October. "I do not need to tell you that I miss you," Harrison wrote. "All the others here have other duties & since you left I have no one to look specially after me."[15]

In many of his speeches, Harrison addressed the tariff issue, which dominated the campaign. In July the Democratic House of Representatives had passed a low-tariff bill; it came under sharp attack in the Senate, where Republicans offered a protectionist alternative. Fearing the power of Republican tariff arguments, President Cleveland tried to reassure voters that Democrats waged "no crusade of free trade" and would exercise "the utmost care for established industries." Harrison, in contrast, felt no embarrassment at his party's program. He insisted that "a protective tariff is constitutional, wholesome and necessary" to "preserve the American market for American producers, and to maintain the American scale of wages." He would apply the revenues generated to internal improvements, aid to education, and reviving the American merchant fleet. Americans, he said, should "not be frightened by the use of that ugly word 'subsidy.'" Moreover, few could miss the reference to Cleveland's pension vetoes when the Republican nominee declared that the government should not "use an apothecary's scale to weigh the rewards of the men who saved the country."[16]

Democrats considered Harrison most vulnerable on labor issues and accused him, falsely, of having said during the 1877 railroad strike that a dollar a day was enough for any workingman. In response, Harrison repeatedly emphasized protectionism's benefits to labor as "the beginning and the end of the tariff question." Nor, he said, should Americans "forget the women who [are] compelled to work for their daily bread." When Democrats said the tariff raised prices, Harrison answered that "those persons who demand cheaper coats would be ashamed of themselves if they could realize that their demand cut the wages of the women who made these coats."[17]

Republicans took other steps to counteract Harrison's "kid-gloves" image. One campaign pamphlet entitled *General Harrison and Labor* featured his arguments in favor of legislation for prompt payment of wages, safety regulations, and arbitration, and against the importation of contract labor. The official campaign biography, written by *Ben-Hur* author and Harrison friend Lew Wallace, gave a benign account of Harrison's actions during the 1877 railroad strike and underscored Harrison's own economic struggles in his early professional life. Harrison gladly accepted the support of Tippecanoe Clubs, groups of old-time voters who had supported his grandfather, but he denied being a wealthy aristocrat. His "good name," he told one such group, "was the only inheritance that has been transmitted in our family." The important thing, he insisted, was to preserve for all Americans the "opportunity which puts the starry sky above every boy's head, and sets his foot upon a ladder which he may climb until his strength gives out."[18]

Overall direction of the campaign lay with the national committee, chaired by Pennsylvania senator Matthew S. Quay. In educating the electorate on the virtues of protection, the Republicans enjoyed help from well-heeled interest groups such as the American Iron and Steel Association, which disseminated millions of protectionist pamphlets. Though Republicans stood united on the tariff issue, some leaders regretted the relative neglect of the traditional Republican defense of black rights in the South. Quay and other strategists argued that with New York and Indiana far from certain, the party should try to carry at least some upper South states, where economic diversification and progress made the Republican tariff stance attractive. Any offensive waving of the "bloody shirt" might deter potential southern converts from voting their economic interest over old sectional prejudices. For his part, Harrison told party leaders that he would not "purchase the Presidency by a compact of silence" on the voting rights question. Instead, he connected the two issues. He argued that white southern economic leaders, who could benefit from Republican policies, should insist on blacks' right to vote and then enlist their aid in working for the adoption of favorable economic policies.[19]

An important component of the Republicans' tariff strategy was to appeal to British-hating Irish-American voters by accusing the Democrats of favoring British notions of free trade. This effort got an unexpected boost from an exchange of letters between George Osgoodby, a California Republican unconnected to the official campaign, and the British minister in Washington, Lionel Sackville-West. Posing as a former British subject named Charles F. Murchison, Osgoodby wrote Sackville-West to express his concern over pending diplomatic issues between the United States and Britain and to ask the minister which presidential candidate would better serve British interests. Sackville-West's naive reply favoring Cleveland found its way into the press. When the British government refused to recall the tactless minister, an outraged Cleveland dismissed him. Although Republicans reveled in the president's discomfiture, the "Murchison letter" seems to have had limited impact. Cleveland increased his share of the vote over that of 1884 in Irish-American precincts in New York and Boston.[20]

As the campaign wound down, allegations of contemplated frauds flew between the Democratic and Republican camps. The near equality in strength of the two parties in Indiana meant that a handful of votes could tip the balance and thus made that state a likelier field for corruption than most others. No less a figure than Robert Lincoln, the president's son, who practiced law in Chicago, told Walter Gresham that Harrison's law partner, William H. H. Miller, and his son, Russell, had come to the city to solicit "money to buy votes." According to Gresham, Lincoln said that he was "in favor of chipping in" because "the democrats were using money the same way."[21]

Early in October, the *Indianapolis Journal* cited a letter allegedly from a Democratic county chairman to a local party operative instructing him to compile a list of voters, to "mark every one who has to have money as a 'float,'" and to "let no one escape." With less than a week to go before the election, the Democrats trumped this charge with a similar one against Republican national treasurer William W. Dudley, himself a Hoosier. The *Indianapolis Sentinel* published a purported letter from Dudley to Indiana county chairmen instructing them to divide the floating voters into "blocks of five and put a trusted man with necessary funds in charge of these five and make him responsible that none get away and that all vote our ticket." A devoted Harrison supporter, Dudley had worked feverishly with Michener at the Chicago convention and had earlier written Harrison, "I love you as a brother and will stand by you as long as I live."[22]

Harrison and national party leaders disavowed any knowledge of Dudley's alleged scheme, and state party leaders denied that Dudley had any role in the Indiana campaign. Dudley had apparently written a letter discussing party organization, which Michener described as containing nothing that was "unusual, illegal or immoral." Dudley denounced the printed version of his letter as a forgery and sued several Democratic newspapers for libel, thereby defusing the crisis somewhat. Nonetheless, Harrison refused to make a public statement exonerating Dudley, and their friendship came to an end. After the election, the Cleveland administration's Justice Department tried to prosecute Dudley, but a Republican federal judge quashed the indictment.[23]

Democrats gleefully played the incident as forever besmirching the holier-than-thou Republican candidate. Still, neither contemporaries nor later historians could be certain about the impact or even the existence of Dudley's and other alleged schemes. Even at the bargain rate of two dollars a vote, neither party had enough money to buy more than a minute fraction of Indiana's half-million voters. The simple fact was that the vast majority of Hoosiers and of the eleven million voters in the nation at large based their choices on long-standing party affiliation or a conception of how each party might serve their interests, or both. In one scholar's view, the Dudley letter so aroused the scrutiny of reporters and poll-watchers that the "election was the cleanest in Indiana in years." Perhaps most important, the *Indianapolis Sentinel,* which had originally printed the "blocks-of-five" letter, conceded that the outcome of the election "must be accepted as a popular verdict against tariff reform and in favor of the extreme protective policy advocated by the Chicago platform." Economics in the broadest sense, rather than a bit of cash in hand, determined most voters' decisions.[24]

Turnout in the election was 79.3 percent—striking evidence of citizens' deep interest in the issues and of the parties' ability to mobilize voters. Harrison carried Indiana by a margin of 0.4 percent and New York by 1.1 percent. These were the only states to shift from Cleveland's 1884 list, but they were enough to put Harrison ahead in the electoral college, 233 to 168. In the nationwide popular vote, Cleveland led Harrison by some 90,000 votes; the Democrats successfully pulled in huge margins for Cleveland in the Deep South, where Republican African Americans were systematically barred from voting. Far more than Dudley's alleged plan for vote buying, southern Democrats' intimidation of African Americans represented the most egregious violation of the franchise in 1888. African Americans favored the Republican Party nearly unanimously, yet since the end of Reconstruction their right to express that preference had steadily eroded. In the two previous decades the black population of South Carolina had grown by more than 60 percent, but between 1872 and 1888 the number of Republican votes cast for president in that state declined by more than 80 percent. Other Deep South states showed similar trends. The tainted character of Cleveland's plurality left the Democrats no moral ground to protest over the popular-vote winner's being denied the presidency; instead, it inspired the Republicans to renew efforts at election reform. Ironically, in the upper South, Quay's strategy of emphasizing the tariff over sectional issues almost paid off; Harrison won at least 49 percent of the vote in Virginia and West Virginia and more than 47 percent in North Carolina and Maryland.

Most important, the Republicans also won a narrow victory in the congressional elections, and for the first time since 1875, the party would hold the White House and both houses of Congress. "It gives you," Blaine wrote the president-elect, "the amplest power for a useful, strong and impressive Administration." Harrison thanked Blaine for his congratulations but confessed a growing "sense of grave responsibilities and shadowy troubles."[25]

A week after the election, Harrison stole a moment to write his first letter without the use of a stenographer. It was to Mame Dimmick: "While I have thought *much* of you and have very many times wished for you, it was hard to find time to write and tell you so. . . . I will not attempt to tell you how I feel. You know that I have been rather oppressed than elated by the thought of success and the realization has not affected me differently." In four months, he would be president of the United States.[26]

# 4

## Centennial President

To govern is to choose, and the first important set of choices a president makes is the selection of his cabinet. He tastes for the first time the power of his position, but he also begins to feel the loneliness of his responsibility. Like most presidents, Benjamin Harrison found selecting a cabinet a trying task. He received abundant advice—some solicited, much unsolicited—but he knew that, as one senator wrote him, "choosing a cabinet is like dying—it is something that nobody can do for you." As a procession of party chieftains made the pilgrimage to Indianapolis to offer their views, Harrison was, as Republican national chairman Matthew S. Quay observed, "all ears and no tongue." Harrison understood the politics involved in assembling a cabinet—the imperative to reward supporters, soothe antagonisms, and temper factionalism—but he acknowledged no obligations in the form of promises or bargains. Above all, he knew that he alone bore accountability for his choices. He must satisfy himself that the men he chose were honest, fit, and amenable to his direction. Withal, he sought advisers who shared his understanding of the national interest.[1]

From the November election forward, it was widely assumed that Harrison would make James G. Blaine his secretary of state. Harrison shared the assumption, but he also recognized that Blaine's appointment could be as troublesome as it was inevitable. The support of the Blaine men in the Chicago convention plus the Plumed Knight's own campaign speeches for Harrison in New York, Indiana, and elsewhere gave Blaine a special claim to recognition. So too did his distinguished record as a former House Speaker, senator, and secretary of state under Garfield. Since the early 1870s, many party faithful had regarded the charismatic Maine leader as Mr. Republican. And therein lay the problem: Blaine's great prestige threatened to overshadow the lesser-known president. Still, given Blaine's capacity for mischief, Harrison concluded that he might "not have so good a time in Washington with Mr. Blaine out of the Cabinet as with him in it." But he was determined to make it clear that this was to be a Harrison administration, not a Blaine administration, that the head of the table would be occupied by the president himself and not by his "premier."

Hence, Harrison delayed asking Blaine to join his cabinet, indeed so long that Blaine began to fairly plead through intermediaries for his old job. Harrison withheld his invitation for more than two months to demonstrate that it came as the president's gift and not as Blaine's entitlement. Harrison knew that Blaine, who was not yet sixty years old and just three years his senior, remained a potential presidential candidate. In offering the State Department position, Harrison stipulated that "each member of my official family will have my *full* confidence and I shall expect his in return." Blaine took the hint. "In becoming a member of your Cabinet," he replied, "I can have no motive, near or remote, inconsistent with the greatest strength and highest interests of your Administration and of yourself as its official and personal head." Time would provide the test of his sincerity.[2]

Harrison found selecting a head for the Treasury Department more problematic. In this era when foreign affairs received far less public attention than did domestic economic issues, such as the all-important tariff and the currency, the secretary of the Treasury played a central role in setting administration policy and in dealing with Congress. Boss Thomas C. Platt of New York had his heart set on the job. Platt's bid rested less on financial acumen than on political clout, and he claimed that the Treasury had been promised to him during the Chicago convention in exchange for New York's support for Harrison. Ominously, in January Platt wrote Louis T. Michener, Harrison's political adviser, that "the whole power of the party in this state, which is able to bring about results, is at my back, and if the President[-elect] does not know it now he should be apprised of that fact." Michener denied Platt's claim about a promise but nonetheless pushed for his appointment on the grounds that the cabinet should include "at least one able political manager."

But Harrison had determined that to give any prominent state boss a cabinet-level appointment would offend civil service reformers. Moreover, Platt's chief factional rival in New York, Warner Miller, also sought the Treasury post, and the president-elect decided that to choose either one would alienate a large portion of the New York party. In the end, he selected a third New Yorker, Benjamin F. Tracy, not for the Treasury but for the Navy Department. The choice proved a fortunate one. Tracy became one of Harrison's most effective secretaries and a close friend. Politically, however, his nomination fell short. Although Tracy had been a stalwart Platt ally and had urged Harrison to name Platt to the Treasury, his own appointment as a reward to New York did not mollify either the boss or his factional opponents.[3]

Another strike against Platt's candidacy was his residence in New York. In the West, agrarian movements advocating an expansion of the national currency were growing in popularity, and this made the appointment of any eastern banker or businessman to the Treasury post politically unwise. Harrison's first choice was Iowa senator William B. Allison, a westerner of essentially orthodox financial views. Much to Harrison's disappointment, the Iowan preferred to stay in the Senate. Harrison next turned to William Windom, a former Minnesota senator who had enjoyed a brief but successful tenure in the Treasury job in the Garfield administration. After leaving the Senate, Windom had engaged in business in New York. Eager to avoid any embarrassment, Harrison personally directed inquiries about Windom's business connections to make certain that he did not stand too close to Wall Street. In mid-February Windom passed muster in an interview with the president-elect, who offered him the Treasury post.[4]

Southern Republicans pushed for representation in the cabinet, and Harrison was open to taking a bold step. For a time, he considered looking for a southerner who had served in the Union army for the job of secretary of war. Another possibility was a southern lawyer for attorney general. But Supreme Court justice John Marshall Harlan cautioned him to find a strong ally for the latter job, because "much that you will aim to do in order to protect the elective franchise against fraud and violence will depend upon the wisdom & efficiency which characterizes the Department of Justice."[5]

In the end, the closest Harrison came to tapping a southerner was his selection of his old college friend John W. Noble, from the border state of Missouri, to be secretary of the interior. A native of Ohio, Noble had commanded an Iowa regiment in the war and had practiced law in Missouri since 1867. To head the War Department, Harrison chose not a southerner but New England marble magnate Redfield Proctor, who had chaired the Vermont delegation in Chicago, where the state had cast all of its votes for Harrison on all eight ballots. For attorney general, Harrison appointed his law partner and longtime friend and political confidant William H. H. Miller. Although Miller's appointment drew criticism, Harrison was determined to have at the cabinet table one individual in whose judgment he had complete trust and confidence.[6]

For postmaster general, Harrison chose Philadelphia department-store king John Wanamaker, who had helped raise some three million dollars for the 1888 campaign. The appointment hardly pleased Quay, who saw Wanamaker as a potential rival in Pennsylvania Republican politics. For the post office, Quay had pushed his vice chairman at the national committee, James S. Clarkson of Iowa, who had to settle for the position of first assistant postmaster general. The newly created Agriculture Department went to Governor

Jeremiah Rusk of Wisconsin. At a crucial point at the Chicago convention, Rusk had abandoned his favorite-son candidacy in favor of Harrison and, later, he had helped raise vital funds for the Indiana campaign.[7]

Harrison had assembled a competent and hardworking team, though one whose members, except for Blaine, were relatively obscure. Past political service certainly figured in several of the choices, but less clear was how well they could deliver future support. Only Blaine himself represented the party's Blaine element, and many of his legions thought that the appointment of only their chief was insufficient recognition. None of the other cabinet secretaries brought to the administration an independent political base of any great significance. Four years later, only half the states from which the original cabinet hailed would give Harrison a majority of their convention votes for renomination. Moreover, Harrison's cabinet selections had disappointed and offended several of the party's most powerful leaders—Platt, Quay, Clarkson, and others—men who had convinced themselves that it was they who had put Harrison in the presidential chair. Harrison was willing to acknowledge their contributions to his victory in 1888, but he also had a strong belief in his own role. Even if he were to agree that to a considerable extent he owed his election to these men, he refused to concede that he owed them his presidency. He would not accept the cartoonists' jape that he was not big enough for his grandfather's hat.

On February 25 Harrison and his family bade Indianapolis farewell. That morning, when Harrison led the family prayers, Caroline's sister Elizabeth Lord wrote, "We all shed tears. . . . He is always so apt in speech either to God or man." Later, his private secretary noted that the "badly broken up" president-elect "was alone in his library for a time and full of tears when the time came to take his leave." The mood continued at the train depot where he told his townsmen, "I love this city." He turned from his "cherished home" of thirty years with mingled feelings of dread, hope, and faith. "There is," he said, "a great sense of loneliness in the discharge of high public duties. The moment of decision is one of isolation. But there is One whose help comes even into the quiet chamber of judgment, and to His wise and unfailing guidance will I look for direction and safety."[8]

Harrison arrived in Washington a week early. He exchanged calls with Cleveland, put the finishing touches on his cabinet, and previewed his inaugural address with Blaine, Windom, and Senate leaders. On Inauguration Day, March 4, rain fell in "torrents," but, as Elizabeth Lord recorded, remembering his grandfather's fate, "Ben had fortified himself with a chamois undersuit" to keep dry. Nor did the downpour dampen the hopes of the assembled Republicans who repeatedly interrupted Harrison's address with applause and cheers.[9] Calling his oath of office "a mutual covenant" with the people, Harrison invoked "the favor and help of Almighty God" to give him "wisdom, strength, and fidelity," and to animate the people with "a spirit of fraternity and a love of righteousness and peace."

The new president considered his inaugural address less an opportunity to purvey platitudes than to prescribe policy. Playing up the centennial theme, he hailed the contrast between the weak thirteen states of Washington's day and the thirty-eight "populous and prosperous" states of his own time. That progress, he suggested, was not mere evolution or happenstance; it reflected the fostering care of government. Invoking the sanction of the Founding Fathers for the Republican economic program, he noted that a nationalist drive for economic independence and self-sufficiency had fueled the formation of the Constitution in the 1780s. Now, after a century, tariff protectionism represented "the same patriotic interest in the preservation and development of domestic industries and the defense of our working people against injurious competition." He urged southerners to accept the protective tariff as an engine for diversity in their stagnant economy. The South should not, he said, let "the prejudices and paralysis of slavery continue to hang upon the skirts of progress."

Harrison declared that the Treasury surplus was "not the greatest evil," but it was a "serious" one. Even so, he rated preserving protectionism much more desirable than penny-pinching frugality. He advocated expenditures to build a stronger navy and to support American commerce through subsidies to steamship lines. He drew the greatest round of applause when he called for more generous pension legislation for Union veterans and their widows and orphans.

Only a small portion of Harrison's address dealt with foreign affairs. In an age when European nations were extending imperial establishments around the globe, he reiterated the Monroe Doctrine's admonition against any such movements in the western hemisphere. Nor would the United States accept control of a canal through Central America by any European power. America's own overseas ambitions would be narrowly circumscribed: "The necessities of our navy require convenient coaling stations and dock and harbor privileges." But, he pledged, "These and other trading privileges we will feel free to obtain only by means that do not in any degree partake of coercion, however feeble the Government from which we ask such concessions."

On the touchy question of patronage and civil service, Harrison said that "honorable party service" would be neither "a disqualification for public office" nor a shield for negligence or incompetence. He conceded that because the federal bureaucracy had grown so large, in making appointments, a president had to rely on the recommendations of others. But, he complained, "these are often made inconsiderately and without any just sense of responsibility." He and the department heads would need "time for inquiry and deliberation." "Persistent importunity will not," he warned, "be the best support of an application for office." His statement that the civil service law would be enforced "fully and without evasion" met a stony silence, save for a solitary "ah" in the Washington crowd.

Harrison then turned to trusts, calling on the nation's "great corporations" to "more scrupulously observe their legal obligations and duties." Otherwise, their illicit behavior would lead the "ignorant classes" to believe "that convenience or a supposed class interest is a sufficient cause for lawlessness." On the South, Harrison welcomed what he saw as a resurgent interest in reforming the election laws. "No power vested in Congress or in the Executive to secure or perpetuate [the right to vote] should remain unused upon occasion."

Harrison closed with a paean to the nation's magnificent abundance, and he reminded Americans of their solemn obligation to preserve republican liberty. "God has placed upon our head a diadem, and has laid at our feet power and wealth beyond definition or calculation. But we must not forget that we take these gifts upon the condition that justice and mercy shall hold the reins of power, and that the upward avenues of hope shall be free to all the people."[10]

After the rain-soaked inaugural parade and the crush of the evening's ball, Harrison and his wife gladly retreated to the private quarters of the Executive Mansion. Both Benjamin and Caroline found great comfort in family life, and they took with them into the White House as many family members as they could. Permanently in residence were daughter Mary McKee and her two children: the president's favorite grandchild, Benjamin Harrison McKee—Baby McKee, as the press dubbed him—and Mary Lodge McKee. Mary's husband, Robert, joined the household only infrequently when his business permitted. Also on hand at the beginning and intermittently thereafter were son Russell Harrison and his wife, May, and daughter Marthena. Before long, Carrie offered a bedroom to her ninety-year-old father, John W. Scott, who had been scrimping along in Washington on a Pension Bureau clerkship.

But all was not sweetness in the cramped family quarters of the mansion's second floor. Carrie's sister Elizabeth Lord, who lived in Washington, soon found the officious Russell "trying to run things at the White House," and his mother felt compelled to scold Russell for his "horrid" behavior. Robert McKee avoided Russell's company whenever he could and wondered whether his wife could stay on if her brother spent much time in Washington. The president himself was already put out with his son for inviting his in-laws to join the presidential party on the train to Washington. Despite these tensions, Harrison found his chief delight in grandson Benjamin. He walked the floor with the boy when he was sick, and Elizabeth Lord was convinced that he was "decidedly spoiling that child" and "letting Benjamin tyrranize [sic] over him so that he do[es]n't get the rest he needs." Grandpa, however, thought his namesake was "a jolly good boy—not a bit spoiled."[11]

Missing from the ménage was Mame Dimmick, Elizabeth Lord's daughter, whose company Harrison had enjoyed the previous summer. The first letter Harrison wrote as president was to Mame, still sojourning in Germany. "You ought to feel very much flattered at how your Uncle Ben thinks of you," Elizabeth wrote to her daughter. Indeed, Mame was "touched" that "although I had been out of sight for nearly five months yet I was still thought of with affection." Son-in-law Robert McKee may well have thought that some of that affection more rightfully belonged to the president's daughter, also nicknamed "Mame." Having spied the envelope addressed to Mrs. Dimmick in Harrison's handwriting, McKee told Elizabeth, "Mamie—your Mamie ought to feel very happy over the fact that she has the first letter the *President* has written." Before long Harrison was writing Mrs. Dimmick that he would be "very glad" to see her. "You know I don't like crowds & only rest when I can get out with a single silent companion. Just now I have none such."[12]

Much of Harrison's distress came from a constant crush of office seekers, for he soon discovered that the vicissitudes of assembling a cabinet were but a prelude. "I do sometimes feel like a hunted animal," he wrote after five weeks in office, "as my walks & drives & even my meals are often taken with those who are wanting something." As the first Republican president since Abraham Lincoln to succeed a Democrat, Harrison found himself besieged by members of his party, hungry for offices at the administration's disposal.

To handle the avalanche of applications and recommendations, as well as all other pressing business, the president had a staff that was ludicrously small by modern standards. For his chief aide, known as the private secretary, he chose newspaperman Elijah Halford. Having worked closely with Harrison during the campaign and transition, Halford had demonstrated loyalty and discretion. His journalist's skills would prove valuable in purveying the administration's message. In the White House, Halford shouldered a burden so enormous that he suffered a three-weeks' physical collapse in the fall of 1889. Besides the private secretary, the staff included an assistant secretary, two stenographers, a telegraph operator, a purchasing and disbursing clerk, two other clerks, two doorkeepers, and four messengers. Unlike later presidents, Harrison had no speechwriter and prepared his state papers himself.[13]

Throughout his career as a soldier, lawyer, and public servant, Harrison had felt a keen sense of personal responsibility for whatever work he engaged to do. He treated his presidential duties no differently. Although he could delegate work, he could not relinquish the conviction that the country would hold him ultimately accountable for his administration's actions. He was, therefore, a hands-on president. He worked closely with his cabinet secretaries in setting policy in their departments; not infrequently he filled in for them when they were ill or absent. At one point, Halford noted in his diary that the president "has practically the details of four Departments to look over (because of the indisposition of the Secretaries)." In January 1891 Windom died, and his replacement, Charles Foster, soon told Halford that "the man to come [to] to find anything out was the President. He knew more than anyone else."[14]

Thus, by design as well as from necessity, Harrison handled a large number of patronage requests personally. How he handled them offended many of the Republican Party bosses. In his prepresidential career, Harrison had played the patronage game assiduously, but like most presidents, he could not resist the sense of transformation that comes with taking the thirty-five-word oath. In the final analysis, he would be responsible for the integrity of his administration. He well understood that, as had happened with Ulysses Grant, the malfeasance of subordinates could sully a chief executive's reputation.

Harrison refused, then, simply to accept the bosses' patronage recommendations with no questions asked. In one early incident, Republican national chairman Matthew Quay handed the president a list of men whom he and his fellow senator from Pennsylvania wanted appointed. When Harrison asked for information about the proposed officials, Quay said that it was not necessary; the two senators vouched for them. As Halford later recounted, Harrison told Quay that he "could not consent to the surrender of the personal responsibility for appointments which the Constitution enjoined, and he would have proper inquiries initiated on his own behalf, and he hoped the result would be to corroborate the judgment of the senators." Such insistence upon his prerogative (and, as he saw it, his duty) did not sit well with the party grandees.

Nor did his brusque manner. As Attorney General Miller, one of his most confidential associates, conceded, Harrison was not "a *cordial* man" with "any except his intimates," and patronage supplicants brought out the worst in his personality. Even his good friend Eugene Hay found that when he visited the White House to recommend an appointment, Harrison did not offer him a chair but "came forward to meet me in the middle of the room [and] addressed me with the formal 'Mister' rather than by my first name as had been his habit. I easily discerned the absence of his usual cordiality and heartily wished I could avoid the interview."

But Hay also maintained that what "gave Harrison the reputation for coldness was merely caution. . . . [H]e was never cold or austere except when he felt the necessity of being so." In his relations with his family and close friends, he was loving and deeply caring. When Halford fell ill, the president took him and his wife into the White House for his convalescence. When navy secretary Benjamin Tracy's house was consumed by fire, President Harrison rushed to the scene and personally administered artificial respiration. He also performed the sad duty of telling Tracy of the death of his wife and daughter, and he gave the secretary a temporary home in the White House to recover from his injuries. "Few men had quicker, warmer, or more delicate sympathies," Halford recalled. But applicants for favors rarely saw that side of him. "I suppose he treated me about as well in the way of patronage as he did any other Senator," Illinois Republican Shelby Cullom recalled, "but whenever he did anything for me it was done so ungraciously that the concession tended to anger rather than to please."

What set Harrison apart as a politician was his determination to separate his personal life and feelings from his official life and responsibilities. In matters of patronage and otherwise, he adhered to a politics that stressed duty and accomplishment over a clublike camaraderie. He later acknowledged that many applicants for office were "generally respectable and worthy men . . . entitled to a respectful and kindly hearing." But, he argued, "at the end of one hundred days of this work the President should not be judged too harshly if he shows a little wear, a little loss of effusiveness, and even a hunted expression in his eyes." If Harrison drummed his fingers while a senator talked about places for his "people," it was because so many more important matters commanded his attention, and he knew that "the urgent public business . . . [must be] postponed or done at night with a jaded mind." Yet he also knew that in that era of personal politics the ultimate fate of that public business was at stake. "No President can conduct a successful administration without the support of Congress, and this matter of appointments, do what he will, often weakens that support." In the end, sheer numbers worked against him. For any given position, a great many applicants offered themselves; much disappointment, if not bitterness, inevitably ensued. Although during his first year and a half in office Harrison devoted four to six hours per day to patronage matters, the effort won him few friends.[15]

Nor did reformers give the president much credit for resisting the presumptuous demands of Matt Quay and others. In late April, during the commemoration of George Washington's inauguration in New York, Harrison had to sit through a sermon by Episcopal bishop Henry Potter, who portrayed the course of American public life as a declension from the Founders' republican aspirations into a "conception of the National Government as a huge machine, exist-ing mainly for the purpose of rewarding partisan service." Sharing her husband's discomfort, Caroline Harrison was "quite crushed" by this view that there "was nothing good or true since Washing-ton lived & all goodness in the government had departed." A few days after Potter's lecture, Harrison appointed the young reformer Theodore Roosevelt to the Civil Service Commission. Even so, Harrison had neither the power nor the inclination to wipe out the spoils system in toto. He and his aides continued to replace legions of Cleveland Democrats with Republicans. Like many other poli-ticians of the era, however, they concluded that the patronage power was less a blessing than a curse. With bosses disaffected, office seekers disappointed, reformers alienated, and Democrats alleging blatant spoilsmanship, the whole enterprise undermined rather than strengthened Harrison's prospects for renomination and reelection.[16]

A chorus of criticism also greeted the administration's early han-dling of Civil War pensions. Harrison intended to request more generous pensions when the Fifty-first Congress convened in Decem-ber, but in the interim, he moved to liberalize the program under existing legislation. To superintend the work, the president appointed James Tanner to be commissioner of pensions. "Corporal" Tanner, who had lost both his legs at Second Bull Run, was a leader in the Grand Army of the Republic and a zealous advocate for veterans. He was a popular choice for the commissionership, but he quickly became a political liability.

Tanner shared Harrison's belief in a liberal interpretation of the pension law, but his enthusiasm for increased benefits outstripped his discretion. In one well-publicized speech, he declared, "For twenty years I have been able only to plead, but now I am thankful that at these finger-tips there rests some power, . . . though I may wring from the hearts of some the prayer, 'God help the surplus.'" Tanner proceeded to stretch the rules in a number of ways and soon ran afoul of interior secretary John W. Noble, whose department housed the Pension Bureau. Noble warned that Tanner's methods violated existing law, but the commissioner remained defiant. Matters reached a head in September 1889 when Harrison met with Tanner and several cabinet members in a contentious White House conference where the exasperated Noble declared that either he or Tanner must go. Later that night, Harrison dispatched an emissary to Tanner's residence to obtain his resignation.

Democrats had a field day with Tanner, depicting him as the personification of Republican recklessness with the people's treasury. Many old soldiers, on the other hand, were angered by the administration's treatment of their favorite. Harrison did his best to repair the damage. He journeyed to Indianapolis for the dedication of the city's Soldiers and Sailors Monument and for the reunion of his old regiment, hoping to rekindle the veterans' sense of comradeship. He insisted that the pension laws should be "liberally construed" but not so far as to enter "the realm of favoritism." As for Tanner's behavior, he asked, "Could any greater harm be done to the cause of progressive relief to our soldiers than to have the country suppose that any administrative officer could modify the law at his pleasure?" Hoping to "avoid a *second* mistake," Harrison was careful in choosing Tanner's replacement; he finally settled on Green B. Raum, another popular but more judicious veteran. Most important, the president called for legislation granting a pension to every veteran of the Union forces who could no longer support himself, whether or not his incapacity derived from his service.[17]

Harrison expected domestic matters such as veterans' benefits and the tariff to be the central focus of his administration, but charting and implementing new policies on these issues had to wait until the convening of Congress in December 1889. Instead, direction of the nation's foreign affairs fell on the president's plate for the first months of his term. During the 1888 campaign, Harrison had said almost nothing about the country's external relations. In his letter of acceptance, he devoted only one paragraph out of twenty to foreign affairs. This ratio reflected the voters' interests and was in keeping with political discourse through most of the second half of the nineteenth century, when Americans concerned themselves primarily with their nation's internal development.

Yet Harrison did have a well-developed sense of where he wished to take the country in its foreign relations. The late nineteenth century witnessed a shift in outlook and purpose in foreign affairs, and Harrison's administration played an important transitional role. Historically, American administrations had, with some exceptions, been essentially reactive, dealing with crises as they arose. Except for the steady expansion to the Pacific shore, American foreign "policy" was defensive and insular, rooted in the protection provided by the two vast oceans. American leaders talked about extending trade and finding overseas markets, but their accomplishments rarely matched their rhetoric. True to his activist notions of government, Harrison thought the nation could—and must—do more. During the campaign, he stressed the protective tariff and its preservation of the home market for American products. But in the one speech in which he briefly discussed foreign affairs, he declared,

> *we do not mean to be content with our own market. We should seek to promote closer and more friendly commercial relations with the Central and South American States.* . . . We do not desire to dominate these neighboring governments; we do not desire to deal with them in any spirit of aggression. *We desire those friendly political, mental, and commercial relations which shall promote their interests equally with ours.* We should not longer forego those commercial relations and advantages which our geographical relations suggest and make so desirable.

James G. Blaine, Harrison's secretary of state, not only agreed with these views but had been their principal Republican advocate at least since his days in Garfield's cabinet. "We have already a pretty full understanding of each other's views," Harrison wrote Blaine while still president-elect. "I am especially interested in the improvement of our relations with the Central and South American States." "I am glad," Blaine responded, "to find myself in heartiest accord with the principles and policies which you briefly outline for your Administration and I am especially pleased with what you say in regard to Foreign Affairs."[18]

But if Harrison and Blaine were ideologically well suited for partnership, temperamentally the "magnetic" secretary and the austere but assertive president were worlds apart. Harrison had long been a Blaine supporter but never a fawning one, nor had he been within Blaine's inner circle. The president now hoped for an association in which the two would show generous mutual respect but still understand the lines of authority. Blaine, however, had trouble adjusting to the new relationship, and superficial cordiality soon masked mutual suspicion. Upon taking office, Blaine had his heart set on making his son Walker first assistant secretary of state, but Harrison felt that he could not give the two top slots in the department to the same family. Although he gave Walker another job at State, which allowed him to assist his father, Blaine and his wife were deeply disappointed. The refusal of the assistantship, said Halford, "resulted in a rankling that never healed."

But the Blaines harbored a contempt for the Harrisons that transcended their disappointment over this clearly unreasonable request. Neither James nor Harriet Blaine could throw off the notion that the Harrisons occupied places that rightfully belonged to them. Blaine's conviction that he had made Harrison president found ample affirmation among his followers and in much of the press. Moreover, the Blaines considered the "Hoosiers" living in the White House their social inferiors. Throughout his life, Blaine had cultivated an air of sophistication and flashy charm, and he privately disdained the president's sobersided demeanor. In family correspondence, Harriet Blaine mocked Caroline Harrison as "her American majesty" and complained that "Harrison is of such a nature that you do not feel at all at liberty to enjoy yourself."

A particularly telling incident occurred in the summer of 1889, when Harrison planned a visit to the Blaine cottage at Bar Harbor,

Maine. Both James and Harriet pleaded with blue-blood Massachusetts congressman Henry Cabot Lodge and his wife to come also, as
Blaine put it, to "aid us in taking care of the great 'White Ele-
phant.'" Afterward, Blaine sent the Lodges photographs of the
occasion for "a good laugh." In one, he told Nannie Lodge, "The easy
& confidential way in which the President seems to hold your hand
is amusing." Although Harrison noted that during his term "no
unpleasant word was ever exchanged" between himself and Blaine
when they were "face to face," both he and Caroline smarted under
the Blaines' treatment. "They are a strange family," Caroline wrote
to her daughter. "You never know whether they are true or not.
There is an air of mystery about them that gives an impression of
cunning."[19]

The problem was not one of mere differences of personal or
social style. What irked Harrison most was what he saw as Blaine's
unwillingness to shoulder his share of the administration's work.
Blaine was in fact in failing health and away from his post in the
State Department frequently and for long periods. The administration was less than two months old when Harrison and his cabinet
traveled to New York for the Washington Centennial, where the
president was expecting the secretary of state to give a speech "to
uphold the credit of the Administration at the Banquet." At the last
minute, however, Blaine backed out, leaving Harrison to fill in.
Thus, while Blaine nursed an "attack of lumbago" in Washington,
Harrison did not learn the subject of his banquet toast until he sat
down at the table and read it in the program. Nonetheless, drawing
on his talent for improvisation, Harrison revised the prescribed
topic, "The United States of America," to "Our Country," struck a
befitting patriotic note, and made his famous suggestion that the
American flag be flown over all the nation's schoolhouses. When
Harrison returned to Washington, Blaine, still in bed, congratulated
him on his "exceedingly apt" address.[20]

Harrison was solicitous of Blaine's health during his long conva-
lescences and was sincerely sympathetic when the Blaines were

devastated by the death of Walker and one of his sisters in early 1890. Still, the workaholic president could not escape the suspicion that the secretary's recurring illness was as much an excuse as a reason for his absences. "There is something very peculiar about his sickness," Caroline wrote to her daughter during one of Blaine's prolonged sojourns in Maine. The Blaines spent every summer at Bar Harbor, primarily because Blaine considered the hot summers in Washington "perfectly odious and to me absolutely unendurable." The Harrisons could escape for only shorter periods to the nearby Maryland mountains or the New Jersey shore, and the president frequently returned to Washington to conduct business, sometimes including the drafting of diplomatic notes for Blaine's signature. Not unnaturally, Harrison became convinced that Blaine received too much credit for work that he himself had performed.[21]

Yet Harrison's relations with Blaine deteriorated over time. In 1889 they still managed to work together with relative ease. As soon as they took office, they confronted their first crisis in a dispute with Britain and Germany over the Pacific island nation of Samoa. American concern for the distant archipelago extended back to the early 1870s. Trade from the United States was negligible, but it had the potential to grow, and the islands offered a way station en route to the large markets of the East.

In 1878 the United States had entered into a treaty of friendship and commerce with Samoa whereby it gained the right to deposit coal for American vessels at Pago Pago. In return, the United States agreed to use its good offices in behalf of Samoa in disputes with foreign powers. Paying heed to this latter provision, successive American administrations grew increasingly wary of greater British and especially German influence in the islands. The accelerating antagonism among the foreign powers was compounded by fighting between rival factions of Samoans. By the late 1880s, German aggressions against the government of Samoa brought Germany and the United States to the brink of war, but in the final weeks of the Cleveland administration, German chancellor Otto von

Bismarck moved to allay the crisis by inviting the other two powers to discuss the issue at a conference in Berlin. The effort for a negotiated settlement received an unexpected boost when a hurricane at Samoa destroyed most of the naval vessels on the scene and several merchant ships as well.

Harrison and Blaine worked together to prepare instructions for the three American delegates to Berlin, and the two men followed the negotiations closely. Harrison recalled that he and the secretary were in "perfect agreement. Every note was submitted to me and discussed." At one point, Harriet Blaine wrote her daughter, "I found the President here going over the Samoan despatches with your Father. He sat all crumpled up, his nose and his boots and his gloves almost meeting, but he was examining those despatches with care and great intelligence, and though I am not drawn to him, I cannot refuse him the homage of respect."

The administration's sine qua non for the conference was the preservation of an independent Samoan nation under the leadership of a king of the people's own choosing. Harrison and Blaine also instructed the American delegates to resist any agreement that derogated U.S. rights at Pago Pago. Moreover, they should guard against any move by the other powers to dominate Samoa. Such dominance would threaten the interests of the United States, especially its growing trade with the East, which was bound to develop even more with the eventual opening of a ship canal through Central America. Harrison regarded an earlier Cleveland administration proposal, which called for the three foreign powers to name a cabinet of three secretaries for the king, as "not in harmony with the established policy" of the American government. Still, he promised to "give weighty consideration to whatever plan the conference may suggest." In the end, he accepted what amounted to a joint protectorate over Samoa, exercised by the United States, Britain, and Germany.

By mid-June, the conference put the finishing touches on a settlement, known as the General Act of Berlin. Designed to check international rivalry and ostensibly secure Samoa's independence, the act was an assumption of sovereignty in all but name by the three powers. It restored King Malietoa Laupepa to power, but it also provided for the three powers to appoint a chief justice, the president of the municipal council of the port city of Apia, and other officials. The act also instituted a variety of taxes, including import and export duties, license fees, and capitation levies.

It was a momentous step. The administration had halted German expansion, but never before had the United States accepted responsibility for the government of a people beyond its own continent. Equally extraordinary, the United States found itself in the sort of "entanglement" with European powers that for a century it had steadfastly shunned. Nonetheless, Blaine was ecstatic over "our complete success at Berlin," and Harrison hoped the act would be "productive of the permanent establishment of law and order in Samoa." Unfortunately, the diplomatic triumph fell short in implementation. The powers had difficulty finding suitable persons to fill the posts of chief justice and municipal council president, and the natives resisted the regime. Britain, Germany, and the United States had to keep warships present to ensure the enforcement of the chief justice's orders and the collection of taxes. By 1899, the situation had grown so irksome that Germany and the United States agreed to divide the islands between them.[22]

When Harrison dispatched the American delegates to the Berlin conference, he sent with them a small staff, including navy lieutenant John F. Parker, the husband of Lizzie Parker, whose sister, Mame Dimmick, was still traveling abroad. It was a small personal indulgence. "I am sure you will enjoy seeing John & Lizzie in Germany," Harrison wrote to Mame. "It gave me great pleasure to send them over to see you." More to the point, he added, "I hope you may be able to come home with them." Despite Harrison's continued pleas, however, Mame did not return to America until late August. Her mother had become gravely ill, and the president personally arranged with federal officials in New York harbor to expedite Mame's landing. "You will be relieved to find your Mother better— after an anxious voyage," he assured her. "When will I see you?"

But Elizabeth Lord had not really improved. Instead of going to

Washington, Mame took her mother to Stamford, Connecticut, and
after a month, moved with her to a hospital in New York. "The confinement," Harrison wrote to his niece, "will wear on you so much
that I will hardly get a chance to see the benefits of your European
trip, as it will be lost before you come to Washington." In early
November, when Caroline and the rest of the family were away, Harrison found himself "for another Sunday the sole occupant of this big
house—about which I wander without any sense of its being a home.
Very often," he wrote to Mame, "I think of the house on Delaware St.
with a sense of regret, and a strong desire to get back there some
time." Soon thereafter, Mame and Lizzie took their mother back to
Washington, where Elizabeth Lord died on December 10. Mame
stayed on with the Parkers in Washington and became a frequent
guest at the White House. In mid-1890, when Lieutenant Parker
received orders to go to Samoa, Lizzie went with him. "This leaves
Mame entirely alone," Mary McKee wrote, "so Papa said to John &
Lizzie that he would look after Mame during their absence."[23]

In the ensuing months Mame Dimmick became ever more
enfolded within the White House family. She helped Caroline with
social duties and correspondence and accompanied her on shop-
ping trips. On one occasion, when the Harrisons invited Mame to
the theater, she asked her aunt about the appropriate dress. The
president intercepted her note and told her she would be sitting "in
the box—front seat—look your very best." She took long walks
with Harrison and in the evenings often played a relaxing game of
billiards with him in the White House. When the president shared
his ruminations on public affairs, she listened quietly and offered
her impressions when asked. She sometimes helped with his correspondence and even had access to the government code by which
she occasionally translated cipher messages for the president. Mame
Dimmick came to enjoy a position unlike that of any other person
in Harrison's family or his official household.[24]

After the Berlin conference, Harrison and Blaine turned their attention nearer to home. More central than Samoa to their reconceptu-

alization of foreign policy was the quest for closer ties with Latin America. During his brief turn as secretary of state under Garfield and Arthur, Blaine had pushed for an international conference of Western Hemisphere nations to consider their common concerns. Legislation authorizing such a meeting finally passed Congress in 1888, and the young Harrison administration eagerly seized on the idea. Some Latin American leaders saw the proposed conference simply as a vehicle for the United States to increase its trade with its neighbors and economic penetration into the region. Though an exaggeration—Blaine was also interested in diminishing conflict in the hemisphere—the charge was warranted. Over the decades, trade with nations south of the border had grown steadily, but Harrison and Blaine were convinced that the potential market was much larger. The presence of Andrew Carnegie, wagon manufacturer Clement Studebaker, bankers Cornelius Bliss and Thomas J. Coolidge, and shipping magnate Charles Flint on the American delegation demonstrated that the president and the secretary literally meant business with the conference. As soon as the Latin American delegates arrived in Washington in early October, they were whisked off on a six-thousand-mile, six-week tour whose unabashed purpose was, as a Guatemalan delegate put it, "to give us an idea of the extensive manufacturing on which they rely for developing commerce."

The delegates met from November 1889 until the following April. Blaine's able service as conference president helped generate an atmosphere of cooperation and common purpose, but he could not entirely subdue the Latins' suspicions of American intentions nor wean them of their ancient European sympathies and economic ties. Despite the evident goodwill, the conference fell short in concrete results. The delegates defeated a proposal for a customs union that would have eliminated trade barriers in the hemisphere; instead, they recommended that nations negotiate individual reciprocity agreements to facilitate commerce. The conference also rejected the idea of a common silver coin for trade within the hemisphere, a controversial proposal about which the American delegates failed to present a united position. The conference formulated a plan for the arbitration of disputes between nations in the region, but the home governments refused to ratify it. The conference's most lasting legacy was the creation of the International Bureau of the American Republics, a medium for the exchange of economic and cultural information, which in the twentieth century evolved into the Organization of American States (OAS).[25]

Harrison gave Blaine high marks for "very hard, successful and brilliant work" during the conference. Meanwhile, during the fall, the president himself was consumed with the preparation of his first annual message to Congress in early December. He began work on the document two months in advance and announced that he would "positively see no one in the afternoons." With scarcely a week left before the paper was due, Halford found his chief frazzled by the work: "At 4:30 he said he was crazy and we went out walking. He said he never cared for office, felt that he had no taste for public life; felt so when [a] Senator and if he could choose to wake up President or [a] lawyer of Indianapolis he would choose the latter." Still, he plugged away. When he finished, Harrison ran the paper by Blaine, who labeled it "a splendid message—clear, comprehensive, direct, and *meaty*." "The President said he felt very much relieved and very grateful to Mr. Blaine for his kind note," Halford observed. Harrison may have been pleased most by Blaine's calling his message "*meaty*," for he was determined to place his own impress on the nation's domestic policy.[26]

# 5

# The Billion-Dollar Congress

Benjamin Harrison's ambition in foreign affairs was more than matched by a desire to reorient much of American domestic policy. As a former senator, he knew that most of what he wanted to accomplish would require congressional action. In working for his goals, he became one of the most engaged legislative presidents in the late nineteenth century. Indeed, he was so eager to get started that he seriously considered calling an early special session of the Fifty-first Congress, which was elected with him in 1888. He ultimately decided against doing so because of uncertainty in the legislature's partisan balance. Republicans had a small but solid majority in the Senate, but their majority in the House of Representatives was razor thin. In the early fall of 1889, two Republican representatives died, and special elections to fill their places would take time. Moreover, at the time Harrison would have to make the call for the special session, the political affiliation of representatives from the new states of Montana, Washington, and North and South Dakota was yet to be determined. The president feared that "any combination of accidents or misfortunes" could "leave us without a Republican quorum at the special session." He decided to wait for the regular session in December.[1]

As was customary, congressional clerks read Harrison's annual message to the two houses on December 3, 1889. Private secretary

Elijah Halford also arranged for the speedy dispatch of the fifteen-thousand-word document to news outlets around the country. In language that was direct, measured, and free of high-flown rhetoric, Harrison outlined his vision for the country. In the brief opening section devoted to foreign affairs, he noted the Samoan success, the ongoing Pan-American conference, and other mostly routine matters. The nation's foreign relations, he said, were characterized by "good will and cordiality," and "the year just closed leaves few international questions of importance remaining unadjusted."

He then moved to the heart of his message, a long list of recommendations for congressional legislation that would fulfill his and his party's campaign promises. No devotee of laissez-faire, Harrison advocated government action on a wide variety of fronts. He called for tariff revision with the preservation of protection; silver legislation that would not unduly inflate the currency; antitrust legislation; regulatory measures to ensure the safety of railroad workers; and, of cardinal importance, legislation to afford greater protection to the right to vote, especially for African Americans in the South. Harrison believed that wise tariff revision could reduce the federal budget surplus, but he also promoted measures that would put much of the burgeoning revenue to good use: increased veterans' pensions, aid to education, internal improvements, subsidies to revive and expand the American merchant marine, and a dramatic increase in the construction of naval vessels. Taking his legislative role seriously, Harrison declared, "The legislation which I have suggested . . . will promote the peace and honor of our country and the prosperity and security of the people."

Halford's old paper, the *Indianapolis Journal*, called the message "a complete refutation of the indecent charge that the entire time of the President has been devoted to dispensing patronage." Speaking for national Republicans, the *New York Tribune* said, "It has the tone throughout of conscious strength and sincerity, and of profound conviction that the people will unwaveringly sustain the National policies to which they gave approval by their votes one year ago." "If," Vermont senator George Edmunds wrote the president, "now Congress will really go to work & *do* the thing, all will be well with the party & country."[2]

That remained a big "if" as members of the Fifty-first Congress settled in. The addition of eight Republican senators from the new western states would give the party a 47 to 37 edge in the upper house. All five representatives from those states were also Republicans, but the GOP majority in the House was still precariously small. In fighting for the Republican agenda, Harrison had a stout comrade-in-arms in Speaker Thomas Brackett Reed of Maine. Like the president, Reed believed that the "danger in a free country is not that power will be exercised too freely, but that it will be exercised too sparingly."

The large Democratic minority in the House, determined to block the Republicans' exercise of power, resorted to the time-honored tactics of obstruction. One was the so-called disappearing quorum, whereby minority members would participate in debate and then refuse to answer a roll call, leaving the House with no quorum to conduct business. On January 29, 1890, Reed moved to break weeks of stalemate by ordering the House clerk to record silent Democrats as present but refusing to vote, and to include their number in the total for a quorum. The Democrats raised a howl and next tried to impede business through repeated parliamentary motions. Again, Reed was ready, declaring such motions out of order. The Speaker's methods sparked a national debate and earned him the sobriquet "Czar Reed," but the Republican majority adopted his rulings as the formal rules of the House. Like the president, Republicans in Congress were determined to act.[3]

They did not wait for Reed to corral the recalcitrant Democrats on the floor. Soon after the session opened, they began to pursue their agenda in various committees. Many regarded the tariff as the foremost legislative priority, and Harrison had hit the subject particularly hard in his message to Congress. For fiscal 1889, he reported a surplus of receipts over expenditures of $105 million, which was more than a quarter of receipts collected. Nearly 60 percent of the revenue derived from customs duties, making the tariff rates the logical place to decrease the surplus. Harrison did not advocate an across-the-board reduction of duties but instead a careful "revision" of the schedules. "These duties," he insisted, "necessarily have relation to other things besides the public revenues. . . . They have a direct relation to home production, to work, to wages, and to the commercial independence of our country, and the wise and patriotic legislator should enlarge his field of vision to include all of these." Moreover, he argued, the protective principle should be "fairly applied to the products of our farms as well as of our shops." To cut the revenues, he urged Congress to place on the free list (items imported free of customs duties) articles that did not compete with American products, eliminate the internal tobacco tax (which southern growers would appreciate), and perhaps also remove the tax on alcohol used in the arts and manufacturing. As for the tariff generally, the president expressed his fervent hope that "any necessary changes will be so made as not to impair the just and reasonable protection of our home industries."[4]

With this mandate before them, the members of the House Ways and Means Committee, led by Chairman William McKinley, began a lengthy investigation. Tariff laws in this era were enormously complex, often running to scores of pages with rates on a huge variety of articles ranging from absinthe to zinc. Inevitably, the political ramifications of tariff deliberations proved as complex as their economic implications. For any given article, producers and consumers generally disagreed about the most appropriate tariff rate or whether there should be any tariff at all. For many commodities, moreover, producers were also consumers, that is, purchasers of raw materials. Thus, a sheepfarmer and a woolens manufacturer would likely have starkly different notions about customs duties on wool and about those on the woolen jacket the farmer needed to buy. Although manufacturing had steadily moved westward with the railroads, factories were still more highly concentrated in the Northeast, with more agricultural regions situated beyond the Appalachians. Tariff discussions could not help but have a sectional dimension. For weeks,

McKinley and his committee held hearings, listening patiently as representatives of diverse interests explained their needs.

McKinley, considered by many a tariff expert, essentially agreed with the central aims Harrison had outlined: reduce the surplus while preserving protection. Over the months, he and his committee worked to fashion a policy that would achieve those goals and be politically palatable as well. Eastern industrial interests could generally count on continued, and in many cases increased, protective rates. But McKinley and his Republican colleagues were particularly concerned about pleasing western farmers. Many farmers who were debt ridden or barely scraping along were joining Farmers' Alliances and threatening to abandon their allegiance to the GOP. In response, McKinley proposed to increase duties on wool and, as Harrison had suggested, to place duties on a raft of other agricultural products for the first time. These new duties would supposedly protect American farmers from competition primarily from Canada and Mexico. More important, McKinley sought to give farmers relief as consumers, especially by putting sugar on the free list. In addition, because the duty on the popular commodity had been one of the most lucrative for the government, letting sugar enter the country free would go far toward cutting the surplus. Paying a bounty to American sugar producers, mostly in Louisiana, who would face increased competition from abroad, would help to reduce the surplus still further.

Although Harrison was generally pleased with McKinley's course, his free-sugar scheme came in for severe criticism from Secretary of State James G. Blaine. The Pan-American conference then in session had rejected a hemispheric customs union and called for bilateral reciprocity agreements instead. Blaine thought a key way to help farmers (and, incidentally, the Republican Party) was to find markets in Latin America for American wheat and hogs and other foodstuffs. Placing sugar, one of the most important imports from south of the border, on the free list by statute would deny the government needed leverage to open the southern markets.[5]

After nearly five months, the Ways and Means Committee presented its bill to the House in mid-April 1890. In his accompanying
report, McKinley generously acknowledged Harrison's leadership,
quoting the president's tariff recommendations in their entirety.
Paraphrasing Harrison's goals, the chairman said that he and his colleagues "have not looked alone to a reduction of the revenue, but
have kept steadily in view the interests of our producing classes."

The bill called for a reduction in some rates and added many
items to the free list. It also called for an increase of duties on many
articles and commodities that competed with American products.
But the generally higher duties would not yield greater receipts,
McKinley insisted. In nearly every case, the increased duties would
"reduce rather than enlarge the revenues, because importations will
fall off." As for the consumer, McKinley said, "We have not been so
much concerned about the prices of the articles we consume as we
have been to encourage a system of home production which shall
give fair remuneration to domestic producers and fair wages to
American workmen." McKinley argued that within the protected
American home market, "increased production and home competition" would "insure fair prices to consumers." Nonetheless, this
seemingly cavalier attitude toward prices handed Democratic
opponents a powerful political weapon. The chief break McKinley's bill gave to consumers was, despite Blaine's protestations, to
take the duty off raw sugar. Sugar was "an article of prime necessity," and "justice as well as good policy" required the removal of the
"unnecessary burden," McKinley said. American sugar producers
would be compensated for the loss of protection by a bounty of
two cents per pound.[6]

Speaker Reed promised the administration that the House
would "get through the Tariff Bill promptly," and he did not disappoint. After two weeks of tightly controlled debate, the House
passed the bill on May 21, 1890, by a vote of 164 to 142. No
Democrat voted for the bill; only one Republican voted against it.
On this central issue, the president's party had maintained unity.

The bill contained no language outlining a procedure for reciprocity negotiations, but Harrison and Blaine remained hopeful that they could secure insertion of such a provision in the Senate.[7]

While McKinley's committee drafted the tariff measure in the winter and spring of 1890, a special House committee chaired by Henry Cabot Lodge labored over another of the president's key initiatives, a bill to reinforce black voting rights in the South. The need for new federal protections was clear to Harrison and other Republicans, and their capture of both the presidency and Congress in 1888 gave them the first opportunity in more than a decade to enact new legislation. At the start of the administration, Attorney General William H. H. Miller lost little time in ordering Justice Department attorneys in several southern states to launch prosecutions for alleged infractions of federal laws during the recent election. But, as in the past, these prosecutorial efforts met stout resistance, and southern juries rarely proved willing to convict or even indict violators of the existing statutes. Frustrated, Harrison and Miller believed that Congress must enact further legislation to render the ballot truly secure.[8]

Harrison gave an eloquent appeal for such action in his annual message. Blacks, he observed, "have their representatives in the national cemeteries, where a grateful Government has gathered the ashes of those who died in its defense." In civil life, African Americans were "now the toilers of their communities, making their full contribution to the widening streams of prosperity which these communities are receiving." And yet, "by various devices," those same communities barred blacks from exercising their political rights.

> When and under what conditions is the black man to have
> a free ballot? When is he in fact to have those full civil rights
> which have so long been his in law? When is that equality of
> influence which our form of government was intended to

secure to the electors to be restored? This generation should courageously face these grave questions, and not leave them as a heritage of woe to the next.

Harrison urged Congress to use "its well-defined constitutional powers" to "secure to all our people a free exercise of the right of suffrage and every other civil right under the Constitution and laws of the United States." That enfranchised blacks would vote overwhelmingly for his party did not detract from the justice of the president's plea.[9]

After studying various proposals, Lodge's committee offered a bill in mid-March. It pertained solely to elections of representatives in Congress, the elections that most clearly fell within Congress's purview to regulate. The bill stipulated that upon the petition of five hundred voters in a congressional district, the federal judge for the district could order that federal officials take over the entire management of a pending election for representative, from registering voters to conducting the vote to counting the ballots. Harrison was skeptical of this approach. Although he had no doubt that Congress had every constitutional right and power to take such a drastic step, the president thought "better results" would come from a strengthening of the existing legislation that allowed for federal supervision, rather than complete absorption, of congressional elections. After two more months of deliberations in committee as well as in party caucuses, Lodge introduced a new bill embodying Harrison's preferred supervisory principle.[10]

Lodge's bill was more than seventy pages long and filled with detail. Previous statutes had called for federal judges, upon petition by citizens, to appoint federal election supervisors in towns or cities of more than twenty thousand population. The new bill would apply the procedure to smaller jurisdictions as well. The supervisors would observe all phases of registering, voting, and counting in congressional elections, and would file a return of vote totals in addition to the tally that state officials made. The bill's most remarkable feature called for a federal board of canvassers appointed by the federal circuit judge in each state and empowered to declare winners according to the supervisors' returns. If the canvassers' decision were challenged, the judge would make the ultimate determination. This was the real heart of the bill. Heretofore, southern Democratic governors or other officials had issued certificates of election; Lodge's bill had the potential to work a fundamental reordering of power in the South.[11]

In the passionate House debate, Democrats fought ferociously against the measure. They branded it a "force bill" that would bring back the horrors of Reconstruction and bayonets at the polling place. Although the bill would reaffirm the president's existing statutory power to use troops to uphold the law, it was most unlikely that any president would take the politically suicidal step of sending troops at election time (and the offending passage was later eliminated in the Senate). As Republican senator John C. Spooner of Wisconsin observed, what southern Democrats really "dreaded and hated" was the thought of losing the power of certification in congressional elections to federal canvassers or a judge appointed by a Republican president. Nor did they hesitate to invoke race. As one Georgia congressman put it, southern whites would not again submit to being "over-ridden and down-trodden by a race whom God never intended should rule over us." But the House Republicans showed equal determination, and they had numbers on their side. Once again, Reed kept a tight grip on debate. The Republican caucus chairman told his colleagues that it was "imperatively necessary" that they be present for the scheduled vote. Nearly all of them were, and on July 2 the House passed the bill by a party-line vote, 155 to 149. Like McKinley's tariff, the federal elections bill was headed for the Senate.[12]

But earlier action in the upper chamber on federal aid to education suggested that Lodge's bill might encounter rough sledding. As a senator, Harrison had given cautious support for proposals to use federal dollars to help educate former slaves and their descendants, and he had reiterated that support in his annual message. The states had made progress, he noted, but "a great work remains to be done, and I think the General Government should lend its aid." For decades, the government had given land grants to fund education; a "direct grant of money from the public Treasury" would be just as useful and just as constitutional. Still cautious, however, Harrison recommended that appropriations be limited in amount and duration so as to relieve states of "the temptation to unduly postpone the assumption of the whole burden themselves."

As it happened, several Republican senators seemed more impressed by the president's caution than by his generosity. New Hampshire senator Henry Blair reintroduced his bill for federal aid, which in previous Congresses had three times passed the Senate before failing in the House. This time, however, the bill lost in the Senate, 31 to 37. Although, counting pairs, Republicans favored it 27 to 18, some thought the price tag—$77 million spread over eight years—was too high. Others, such as Spooner and Ohio's John Sherman, thought that on the controversial southern question, Republicans should concentrate their energies behind the elections bill. Whether they could assemble a Republican majority for that bill in the Senate, however, remained an open question.[13]

On two other issues, veterans' pensions and trusts, the Senate as well as the House moved expeditiously to endorse President Harrison's recommendations. As a senator, Harrison had fought for pensions for all ex-soldiers unable to support themselves, regardless of the origin of their incapacity for work. Grover Cleveland had vetoed such legislation, but now Harrison insisted that these veterans deserved a "generous provision" from "the nation they served so gallantly and unselfishly." Congress responded with the Dependent Pension Act, which granted an invalid veteran a pension of up to $12 a month, or in the event of his death, pensions to his widow and children or his parents. Before the end of Harrison's term, pension spending reached $144 million annually, more than 40 percent of the federal government's receipts. Later scholars of the origins of government welfare policy have called the Dependent Pension Act "watershed legislation."[14]

The Sherman Anti-Trust Act proved even more pivotal. The

growth of big business in the late nineteenth century sparked mixed feelings among Americans. They were proud of the burgeoning capacity of the nation's industries and gladly took their abundant products. Yet the aggressive consolidation of business into larger and more powerful units rekindled Americans' long-standing animosity for monopoly. Politicians scored points promising action against the new combinations, often referred to by the generic term "trusts." Common law and some state statutes offered some legal recourse against unfair combinations, but the late 1880s witnessed a growing sentiment that the vast size of some of the new consolidations called for federal action. The platforms of both major parties in 1888 condemned trusts and combinations.

Although the American principles of federalism raised some doubt about what the national government could do to regulate businesses incorporated by the states, Harrison nonetheless urged Congress to explore "how far the restraint of those combinations of capital commonly called 'trusts' is [a] matter of Federal jurisdiction." Harrison had no intention to reverse the evolution of American economic enterprise, and he counted many industrialists, including Andrew Carnegie, among his friends. But he did believe that it was time for the federal government to play a greater role in policing the behavior of the emergent big businesses. "When organized, as they often are," he declared, "to crush out all healthy competition and to monopolize the production or sale of an article of commerce and general necessity, they are dangerous conspiracies against the public good, and should be made the subject of prohibitory and even penal legislation."

The day after Harrison's message was read, Senator John Sherman introduced an antitrust bill, virtually identical with one he had sponsored in the previous Congress. Like Harrison, Sherman had originally wanted to outlaw monopolization in "production" as well as trade, but debate revealed a prevailing belief in Congress that the Constitution limited the federal government's jurisdiction to business practices related to matters of interstate or foreign commerce. After considerable amendment, the final version of the bill outlawed every contract, combination, trust, or conspiracy "in restraint of trade or commerce," and it imposed fines of up to five thousand dollars (equal to an entire year's salary of a member of Congress) and up to a year in prison. In this form the bill won approval with only a single dissenting vote. Although it may not have been all that Harrison had wanted, it was "prohibitory" and "penal." He signed it on July 2, 1890.

The unanimity of support could not mask the sense most participants felt that the new law was in large measure experimental. Within months, the Justice Department won its first case, involving price fixing by coal companies in Tennessee. Still, prosecutions were slow in coming, and one year after Harrison signed the law, Attorney General Miller felt the need to explicitly advise federal attorneys to lay the law "alongside any combinations or trusts within your district, and if, by such measurement, it is found that those trusts or combinations are infractions of the law, prosecute vigorously." Later critics faulted the administration for not pursuing trusts more energetically, but in the 32 months remaining in Harrison's term after the act's passage, the administration initiated seven suits; during the 102 months that his two successors were in office, the Justice Department launched only eleven. Although the full potential of the Sherman Act—augmented later by further legislation and court decisions—was not realized until the twentieth century, the bill Harrison signed proved to be one of the most enduring legacies of his administration.[15]

If the antitrust act passed with relative ease, another piece of legislation that bore John Sherman's name, the Silver Purchase Act, taxed Harrison's legislative leadership skills to the limit. The currency question had vexed American politics since the end of the Civil War. In the late 1870s, the government resumed the payment of specie for greenbacks, which thus became a permanent element in the nation's currency. But the volume of greenbacks was finite, and those who wished to expand the money supply turned to silver. Through much of the nineteenth century, silver had formed an insignificant part of the country's circulating medium, and in 1873 the government ceased coining silver dollars. But the discovery of large deposits of the white metal in the West sparked calls for its "remonetization," not only from silver producers but from inflationists who saw renewed silver coinage as a way to revive a depressed economy. In 1878 the Bland-Allison Act renewed a limited coinage, stipulating that the Treasury should purchase and coin between two million and four million dollars in silver each month. In the ensuing years, the Treasury purchased only the minimum amount, disappointing silver advocates.

In his prepresidential career, Harrison had posted a conservative record on the currency question, arguing for the necessity of keeping paper and silver money equal to gold. But the issue divided both major parties, and Harrison had decided to say little about it in his drive for the presidency in 1888 and in his inaugural address. In the months before Congress convened, however, the movement for greater coinage accelerated, fueled by a stringency in the nation's money market that hurt debtors and farmers wishing to move their crops. What the silverites wanted was for Congress to throw off the Bland-Allison restraints and enact the free and unlimited coinage of silver at the current legal ratio of 16 to 1 with gold. Indiana Republican chairman Louis T. Michener, who served as the administration's political eyes and ears, urged Harrison to address the issue in his annual message, because, he said, the Farmers' Alliance "has declared in favor of free coinage of silver, and that means disaster to the Republican party unless we have very wise legislation."[16]

In his message, Harrison offered a balanced discussion of the currency issue, although it was clear that he did not believe that "wise legislation" included free coinage. Since 1878, the nation's money supply had grown by six hundred million dollars, or about five dollars per capita, and more than half the growth derived from silver coin or certificates based on coin. Thus, Harrison conceded, the "evil anticipations which have accompanied the coinage and use of the silver dollar have not been realized." But, he added, the Treasury had never purchased more than the two-million-dollar minimum of silver because of the continued disparity between the silver dollar's face value and its bullion value, which was now about seventy-two cents per coined dollar. Under the operations of the classic monetary principle of Gresham's law, that disparity could easily drive gold out of circulation and put the country on a single silver standard. Free coinage of silver or indeed "any considerable increase of the present rate of coinage" would accentuate "the difference in the bullion values of the gold and silver dollars" and jeopardize the equitable use of the two coins. "Such a result," said Harrison, "would be discreditable to our financial management and disastrous to all business interests." "Any safe legislation upon this subject," the president insisted, "must secure the equality of the two coins in their commercial uses." Harrison was strongly advocating the preservation of the gold standard.

Still, Harrison signaled to the silverites his willingness to seek common ground. He endorsed a plan devised by Secretary of the Treasury William Windom that called for the Treasury to purchase silver and pay for it not with coined dollars but with new Treasury certificates. The dollar price paid in certificates would not reflect any fixed ratio between the two metals but would instead be based on silver's current market price vis-à-vis gold. Similarly, the certificates would be redeemable in gold or in a quantity of silver bullion according to its current market price in gold. In essence, this bullion redemption provision would make silver only a representative of gold, eliminating the threat that free silver coinage could pose to the economy. This approach, said Harrison, would "satisfy the purpose— to continue the use of silver in connection with our currency and at the same time to obviate the danger" of going off the gold standard.[17]

In drafting legislation to enact the plan, Harrison and Windom recognized that it had implications beyond the economics of the silver question. Pro-silver Republicans potentially held the balance of power in each house of Congress. They could determine the fortunes of other items on the administration's agenda, such as the tariff and the elections bills. Although Harrison could not accede to the silverites' *beau ideal*—free coinage—he hoped to mollify westerners and forestall a revolt on other issues. In addition, he hoped to resolve the party-rending currency question well in advance of the November 1890 congressional elections. Republicáns, rather than Democrats, should be the ones to assume the credit for successful silver legislation.

By mid-January, Windom had prepared a bill embodying his plan. Harrison approved, and it was introduced in both houses. No sooner had he learned the contents than Colorado Republican senator Henry M. Teller, a leading silver advocate, rushed to the White House to register his dissent. Teller found Harrison not inflexibly committed to the text of the measure as it stood, but the president made clear to the senator that "what he wanted was a Republican law and one he could approve." He warned Teller that he would veto a free-coinage bill. Strong as they were in the Fifty-first Congress, the silverites (Republicans and Democrats) could not muster a two-thirds vote to override a veto. In the ensuing six months of tangled negotiations, Harrison's absolute refusal to sanction any measure for free coinage exercised a potent influence on the shape the legislation ultimately took.[18]

The administration kept close tabs on the progress of the bills in Congress. Windom traveled to Capitol Hill several times to defend his handiwork. Preferring to lobby behind the scenes, Harrison gave a series of White House dinners for small groups of senators and representatives, occasions that came to be known as "Ben Harrison's Silver Dinners." At these intimate affairs, which sometimes went on until midnight, Halford wrote, the president made it clear that he was "anxious to secure some compromise that would unify the party and satisfy the country." According to the House Republican caucus chairman, Harrison's "dinners were the wisest thing that could have been done."[19]

But the silverites in Congress would not give in without a fight, and the struggle dragged on into June. As one congressman described the contending camps, "You might as well expect the Laplander and the Hottentot to exchange residences and then each insist that the climate of his new home was delightful." The key sticking point was Windom's proposal for the redemption of silver certificates in bullion, which silver advocates saw as "a surrender to the mono-metallic gold standard." In private meetings, Harrison argued for the bullion redemption clause, yet he also indicated that keeping free coinage out of the bill was the only point on which he would not budge.

On June 7 the House passed a modified version of Windom's plan. Unlike the secretary's proposal, the House bill set an exact fig-ure for silver purchases, $4.5 million per month, but, with the House firmly in Speaker Reed's grip, the silverites were unable to eliminate the bullion redemption clause. After a brief debate, the bill passed, 135 to 119. Voting yes were 134 Republicans and 1 Union Laborite. No Democrats voted for the bill, and only 7 Republicans voted against it.[20]

A majority of Senate Republicans saw the House bill as the basis for a settlement, but its silverite Republican opponents were vocif-erous. Condemning administration interference in Congress's work, Colorado's Edward Wolcott said that Harrison was "unmindful of the interests of the country" and had used "the sunshine of execu-tive patronage" to secure support for his position. The *Indianapolis Journal* labeled the attack "indecent," but Wolcott and his allies won the next round. In a surprise move, the Senate silverites presented a substitute bill for free coinage at sixteen to one, which carried by a vote of 42 to 25. Fifteen Republicans favored the bill, while 22 voted no. Huddled with advisers at the White House, Harrison thought "the Senate had dealt the Party a bad blow."[21]

But he did not give up. His family had gone to Cape May, New Jersey, for the summer, but Harrison stayed in Washington, continu-ing to lobby. "I have some members or Senators to dine with me informally almost every ev[enin]g," he wrote to Caroline. He also used the press to emphasize that he favored "a judicious silver bill" that would increase the currency but not one that would "be objec-tionable to any considerable section of the country." Privately, Hal-ford described Harrison as "quite resolute."

Lining up with the president, the House rejected the Senate's free coinage amendment by a vote of 135 to 152, thereby necessitating a conference. Only 22 Republicans voted for the bill, while 130 Republicans voted no. Reed and other House GOP leaders had done their work well in holding the party together but so also had the president. Illinois Democrat James R. Williams charged that Harrison "has sent to members of this House his intimation threatening the Senate bill with a veto." Unlike the Republicans, Williams declared, "I do not propose to go to the President of the United States and get down on my knees and ask him what kind of silver legislation he is in favor of." But Harrison was delighted with what he and the "strong man" Reed had accomplished. "We had a great success yesterday in getting the silver bill into conference," he wrote to Mame Dimmick at Cape May. Although he was eager to join the family at the shore, he thought "I ought to stay where I can confer with any who may want to see me about the terms of the compromise." "Love to all," he added hastily. "Some Senators are waiting."[22]

Under the leadership of John Sherman, the Republican members of the conference committee hammered out a draft. While Sherman and Nevada senator John P. Jones sparred over the amount of silver to be purchased, the Senate's silver Republicans threatened to hold other important bills hostage. At one point, they joined the Democrats in blocking a motion to take up the tariff bill, prompting one Senate clerk to predict that both the tariff and the elections bill "will have to go unless they get all they ask in the direction of free coinage." The silver Republicans did not get all they wanted, but they got a bill they could vote for.

The conference bill expressed the silver to be purchased not as 4.5 million dollars' worth but 4.5 million ounces per month, to be paid for by certificates. It was an amount that approximated the entire U.S. output and was designed to please the silver producers. The bill omitted the bullion redemption clause, but it did stipulate that the secretary of the Treasury could redeem the certificates "in gold or silver coin, at his discretion" and further that it was "the established policy of the United States to maintain the two metals on a parity with each other." This latter phrase was the glue that held the compromise together. It was vague enough to give heart to silver advocates that gold and silver would be treated equally, but in fact the clause served to buttress the gold standard by authorizing the secretary to redeem the silver certificates in gold rather than silver. Sherman had succeeded in placating Republicans all along the spectrum. The Senate approved the bill by a party-line vote of 39 to 26. The House followed suit, 122 to 90; voting yes were 121 Republicans and 1 Union Laborite; Democrats cast all the no votes.[23]

At the White House, Halford wrote in his diary, "The President was feeling very good and all our friends were jubilant." Passage of the bill, Harrison wrote to Caroline, "was very gratifying to all our people. I have been asking for a Republican bill and this must be one for no Democrat voted for it in either House. It is not just as I wanted it, but it is not so far away but that I shall be glad to end a controversy by signing it." Sign it he did, with Windom standing by, on July 14. From the president's hometown, the *Indianapolis Journal* declared, "There has been no greater triumph for the Republican party for years than this unanimous passage of the silver bill."[24]

Harrison could not rest on these laurels, however, for other important legislation, including the tariff and elections bills, still awaited action in the Senate. When the Finance Committee reported McKinley's bill with sugar still on the free list, Harrison and Blaine launched a campaign on the advantages of reciprocity. The president sent a special message to Congress and forwarded Blaine's report on the International Conference of the American States, which elaborated the argument for reciprocal exchanges. In June Blaine pushed the idea in person with senators at the Capitol and provided draft reciprocity amendments for the McKinley bill. Through much of the summer, one observer noted, "The President made little dinner parties, in order to bring the leading Republicans together for conference and discussion, with a view of bringing about an agreement between the contending parties and securing tariff legislation."[25]

As Congress weighed reciprocity, sugar remained a central point of contention. Some favored putting sugar on the free list with the proviso that if sugar-exporting countries did not admit American products free of duty, the United States would reimpose a sugar duty. Others said a duty should be kept on sugar to be removed only after other countries agreed through negotiation to remove their duties on American goods. Although Blaine found either method acceptable, his public rhetoric showed a clear preference for the latter course.

When Harrison discussed the issue with Republicans in Congress, he concluded that they would not take sugar off the proposed free list. As they looked toward the fall congressional elections, the Republicans saw that, given the McKinley bill's general increase of duties, popular pressure for free sugar was simply too great not to enact it. Nonetheless, Blaine, who escaped to Bar Harbor in early July, wrote a public letter denouncing free sugar without some reciprocity provision as "unwise." Harrison, who stayed in Washington, knew that a successful proposition must take congressional Republicans' concerns into account. He admonished Blaine that they could not avoid free sugar but reported that he was devising an amendment whereby "we can still hold the string in our hands" for reciprocity agreements. Blaine remained skeptical. Without clearing it with the president, the secretary issued another public letter asserting that the "only danger" to advantageous reciprocity agreements was the push in Congress "to open our ports free to everybody's sugar, and to do it with such rapidity that we are not to have a moment's time to see if we cannot make a better trade." After this second letter, Blaine wrote to Harrison, "I hope I have said nothing that you think had better have been left unsaid."[26]

In fact, Blaine's blasts from Bar Harbor did make the president's delicate work in Washington more difficult. "There is some heat and temper among our people in the House growing out of Mr. Blaine's letters, which I am trying to allay & to bring about an agreement," Harrison wrote to Mame Dimmick. To help with the negotiations, he tried to get Blaine to return to the capital for a few days and even offered him quarters at the White House, but Blaine declined.

("I do not wish to be outside of New England for the summer months," Blaine wrote Nannie Lodge.) In early August Blaine did consent to meet with Harrison for a few days in Cape May, where the president explained his reciprocity plan. Working with congressional leaders, especially Rhode Island senator Nelson Aldrich and Maine congressman Nelson Dingley, Harrison had drafted an amendment, the substance of which Aldrich formally submitted to the Senate a few weeks later. It stipulated that sugar, molasses, tea, coffee, and hides would be among the items on the free list but that if the president found that any country exporting those articles to the United States imposed what he deemed "reciprocally unequal and unreasonable" duties on the importation of American products, he could reimpose duties on the enumerated foreign imports. Senate Republicans defeated a proposal to have Congress rather than the president reinstate the duties and thus retained in the amendment what amounted to an extraordinary expansion of executive power over taxation and trade. The Harrison-Aldrich amendment satisfied Republicans and it remained a part of the bill when it finally passed. As Dingley later recalled, he and other Republicans "did not know what they would have done if it had not been for President Harrison."[27]

After he returned from Cape May to Bar Harbor, Blaine wrote to the president, "I could no more endure what you have done this summer than I could create a new world." Harrison longed to join his vacationing family, but his troubles with Congress were not over. After a quick trip to Boston to address veterans at the national Grand Army encampment, he returned to Washington to deal with yet another crisis involving the tariff. For weeks, low-tariff Democrats who opposed the McKinley bill's high protectionism had used all sorts of parliamentary foot dragging to slow its consideration. Businessmen and farm spokesmen increasingly voiced their concern that prolonged uncertainty on the tariff injured all economic interests, and Republicans cast about for ways to circumvent the Senate's time-honored traditions of debate. Senator Matthew Quay, the Pennsylvania boss with close ties to industrialists, concluded that the best way to persuade Democrats to scale back the tariff debate was to alleviate their fear of election legislation after the McKinley bill passed. On August 12, after conferring with Democratic leaders, Quay proposed a resolution to set a definite date to end the tariff debate and postpone consideration of nearly all other pending bills, including the House elections bill, until the next session of Congress. Quay's aim was to stanch the tariff debate through a combination of Democrats who adamantly opposed the Lodge elections bill with those Republicans who gave the tariff a higher priority than the elections legislation.[28]

Quay's move stunned proponents of the elections bill, including Harrison. "There have been some very annoying and discouraging things of a public nature since my return," he wrote to Mame Dimmick from Washington. So discouraged was he that he was tempted to "quit fretting & let things take their way." But, he added, "It is hard to see our advantages wasted." He could not let the Republicans' first opportunity in fifteen years to enact new civil rights legislation be lost without a fight. The president summoned several senators to the White House, and newspapers described him as "leaving no stone unturned to let the Republican Senators know that he wants the Force bill passed." He told each one who met with him that voting for the bill was his "highest duty." In addition, the White House worked on garnering public support by distributing to the press extracts from Harrison's inaugural address and annual message endorsing elections legislation. "It can be authoritatively stated that President Harrison's views have undergone no change whatever," reported Perry Heath, the Washington correspondent of the *Indianapolis Journal*, who was close to both Harrison and Halford. "He believes in a federal election bill, and is very deeply concerned in the prospect of a failure to pass the bill."[29]

The administration's united front was again compromised when rumors circulated through Washington that Blaine had ghostwritten the Quay resolution. Privately, Blaine told Lodge that the charge was untrue. He confessed, however, that he did "not have great faith" that the elections bill would work in removing a disease that, "deepseated and poisonous as it is," would "have to be left to self-cure." On Capitol Hill, Republican Senate caucuses degenerated into shouting matches between the Quay forces and backers of the bill, led by George F. Hoar of Massachusetts and Wisconsin's John Spooner. The principal leverage wielded by the bill's proponents was the unwillingness of most Republicans to go on the record as seeming to oppose elections legislation by voting for Quay's scheduling resolution. Finally, after days of impassioned disagreement, Republicans in caucus reached an understanding. Quay agreed not to press his resolution, thereby obviating an embarrassing vote, and Republican senators pledged themselves in writing to take up the Lodge bill on the first day of the next session, less than four months away, and keep it before the Senate to the exclusion of other matters until it was settled by a vote. The maneuver cleared the logjam. The Senate passed the McKinley bill on September 10, and Quay's resolution was quietly dropped.[30] Lodge bill sponsors such as Spooner remained confident that the signed pledge made it "absolutely certain" that the bill would pass during the next regular session. Less sanguine, black leader Frederick Douglass asked Hoar, "What if we gain the tariff and many other good things if in doing it the soul of the party and nation is lost?"[31]

Harrison and his family spent most of September 1890 on vacation in Cresson Springs in the Pennsylvania mountains. The traveling White House staff comprised Halford and a stenographer, and two wire service reporters went along as well. From his cottage, the president had a direct telegraph line back to the White House. He encouraged congressional leaders to use the dispatch office at the mansion to keep him informed regarding the progress of the tariff and other bills in the closing weeks of the session.[32]

Harrison also used the line to respond to a sharp stringency that struck the nation's money markets in mid-September. Disordered financial conditions abroad, especially in England, had troubled American money and equity markets for some time. The September stringency also reflected the heightened seasonal demand for cash to move crops. When the money market tightened, Harrison and Treasury officials acted swiftly, injecting more than fifty million dollars into the economy through bond purchases, early payment of interest on bonds, and increased pension disbursements. Within a week, Halford was able to report to the cabinet in Washington that "the financial situation has been very considerably, if not entirely relieved." In the absence of the Federal Reserve System, which would not come into being for another quarter century, the administration had performed much as a central bank and had successfully averted a panic. As a sympathetic analyst later wrote, "All this shows that the President is as much of a financier and as great a practical banker as he is a legislator. . . . He was ready to invent new methods for dealing with the most vexatious questions."[33]

While in Cresson, Harrison made a few public appearances in the area, including a visit to Johnstown, scene of a devastating flood soon after he had taken office. In the wake of the disaster, the president had offered federal assistance to the state's governor and had personally spearheaded an effort to raise a relief fund. Now the entire population of the recovering town, with "bells ringing and whistles blowing," turned out to show their gratitude.

He also found time for relaxation at Cresson. Most of the family was there, including Mame Dimmick, with whom the president enjoyed vigorous walks. At one point, when Mame was writing a letter to her sister, she left her writing table to attend to three-year-old Ben. When she returned, she discovered that Harrison, obviously in a relaxed mood, had written on her letter: "Mame has been a tolerably agreeable girl." In a subsequent letter, Mame wrote to Lizzie in Samoa that "Uncle Ben . . . wanted to know whether you had adopted the national dress."[34]

When the Harrisons returned to the White House in late September, Mame remained with them. The house had undergone redecoration in their absence and was still in some disarray but, as Mame wrote, it was "much improved in the living part." Caroline Harrison had made her special cause the expansion of the Executive Mansion to make it a fitting residence in both size and style for the nation's head of state. Although Congress refused to fund expansion, it did pay for major refurbishing, including the installation of electricity. Not long after the return from Cresson, Harrison took over Elijah Halford's small office and gave up his own large office to be used as a family parlor. "How we do enjoy the sitting room, which is being made as home like as possible," Mame Dimmick wrote. "Aunt Carrie seems to depend upon me so and wants me with her all of the time."[35]

On September 30 Congress at last passed the McKinley Tariff bill. "As to reciprocity," Halford noted in his diary, "the fact is that the President is the originator and the promoter of the scheme as it now stands." The bill was one of many Harrison approved in a marathon bill signing at the Capitol on October 1. The tariff, silver, pension, and antitrust laws were only the best known of a host of measures Congress had passed. In late July Harrison had sent what Halford described as "a stinging Anti-Lottery message" to Capitol Hill. Seven weeks later, he signed an act banning the notorious Louisiana Lottery and similar companies from using the mails. When European countries moved to protect their farmers by banning the importation of American meat products on the grounds that they were diseased, the administration launched negotiations to get the bans lifted. In August Congress lent its aid with the Meat Inspection Act, which empowered the Agriculture Department to inspect all meats for export and also authorized the president to cut off imports from countries that discriminated against American goods. With this added leverage, the administration secured an end to the European restrictions by the end of 1891. Early in the session, navy secretary Benjamin F. Tracy, concurring in the ideas of naval strategist Alfred Thayer Mahan, recommended appropriations for a vastly expanded navy, and Harrison emphasized the need for a "rapid increase in the number of serviceable ships." Congress complied with authorization for six new vessels, including three coastline battleships, larger than any in the navy's history, at a cost of six million dollars each.[36]

Congress adjourned on October 1, after one of the longest and most productive sessions in its history. That day, no doubt reflecting her uncle's feeling, Mame Dimmick wrote to her sister that "there has been more work done in Congress and by the President and Cabinet than for twenty years." The sentiment ranged beyond the White House sitting room. Newspapers and party spokesmen hailed the first session of the Fifty-first Congress for its "unprecedented record." Future House Speaker Joseph Cannon praised Harrison as a "radical in the matter of legislation" who "has kept the promises of the Republican platform." Ohio congressman Charles Grosvenor gave particular credit to Harrison "as the bulwark of our encouragement, our support and our leadership. All these great measures were outlined in his message to Congress," Grosvenor told an Ohio audience. "All these great measures were advocated by him in his private intercourse with members of Congress." Even so, Harrison was not fully satisfied. As he began preparations for his second annual message, he asked the clerk of the House for a report on the status of all "*important public* measures" still pending. This information would reinforce his recommendations at the opening of the next session.[37]

Before that session convened, however, voters in the midterm elections would pass judgment on what Harrison and the legislature had done. Republicans naturally believed that their achievements had earned them renewed control of Congress. In September they had won a big victory in Maine, where Reed and his three House colleagues garnered large majorities. But the predictive value of the Pine Tree State outcome was uncertain. On the stump, Democrats vehemently denounced the Republicans' activism. They condemned what they considered the extravagance of the "billion-dollar Congress." Even though the Lodge bill had not yet passed, Democrats raised the specter of a revived Reconstruction. On the tariff, they portrayed the Republicans as servants of trusts and warned of skyrocketing prices.

The great imponderable in the election was the farmers' movement burgeoning in the South and the western Midwest. By mid-1890, the Farmers' Alliance claimed more than a million members, and GOP strategists feared defections to third parties particularly in the Republican areas of the Midwest. Harrison himself took the unusual step of making a speaking tour through the region in early October to try to stem the losses. Although he thought the dignity of his position required him to address broad patriotic themes rather than specific issues, several of his speeches suggested a subtext claiming that the nation was enjoying a general prosperity due in large measure to Republican policies. At several points, he particularly urged farmers not to lose hope at temporary setbacks such as short crops. He warned them not to be tempted by "unsafe expedients." In his last speech, in Alliance, Ohio, he made the point clearly: "You should choose such men to represent you in the Congress of the United States as will faithfully promote those policies to which you have given your intelligent adhesion." According to party strategist Louis Michener, "The President's trip did great good everywhere." On the eve of the November election, Harrison decided to return to Indianapolis to cast his ballot "for friends who have done much more for me and for what I believe to be the cause of righteousness and good government."[38]

Righteous or not, however, the cause fell. The voters dealt the Republicans a devastating blow, cutting their representation in the House to a mere 88 seats to the Democrats' 235. At a time when Americans had long been accustomed to little activity at the federal level, Harrison and the Republicans had governed, and now the Democrats seemed to have convinced the electorate that they had governed too much. Afterward, while many Republicans engaged in hand-wringing, Harrison tried to put the best face on the result. He considered the outcome a "disaster," but he did not believe that it represented a rejection of his party's policies or a permanent shift in the electorate. After a few weeks' reflection, he wrote a Hoosier friend, "I have not been so much depressed as many, not because I am an optimist naturally—for I am not—but because it seems to me to be apparent that the influences that operated against us in this election were casual and temporary." He thought that if the

Farmers' Alliance continued to drain Republican strength in states such as Kansas and Nebraska, "our future is not cheerful," yet he also believed that "All such secret organizations are . . . shortlived." Unlike many Republicans, Harrison did not assign much blame to the McKinley Tariff, since the party had done well in some areas with protected interests and had lost in others.

Harrison did blame Republican apathy and division. Some Republicans, he thought, had been less than energetic because of lingering soreness over patronage squabbles or factional fights within their state parties. In some states, such as Massachusetts and Minnesota, he thought that the party had nominated weak men to head the state tickets. In Wisconsin, he noted, many immigrant voters had recoiled against a Republican-passed state law mandating the use of the English language in private as well as public schools. In short, he insisted, the causes of Republican defeat tended to be local and transitory, not national or lasting. "I do not believe the Democratic Party has grown in the confidence of the country, nor been augmented by any permanent accessions."[39]

Harrison's reference to lingering soreness was a tacit recognition that he himself bore some responsibility for the party's loss. Many party leaders, especially those whose hopes for office or patronage influence had been frustrated by Harrison, had no doubt as to his culpability. After the election, Blaine loyalist Stephen Elkins wrote to Whitelaw Reid that "the course of the President since he came into office had much to do with the result—more than appears on the surface." By disappointing "the expectations of the leaders," he had "chilled the party," which "went into this campaign utterly demoralized." Elkins believed the Republicans would have "no chance whatever in '92" unless Blaine "shall consent to lead our forces." As for Blaine himself, he remained on cordial terms with Harrison, although he wrote to Nannie Lodge, "I am afraid you will return to Washington with less admiration for the President if possible than you entertained for him when you set out for New England."[40]

In the week after the election, a near panic again struck financial markets, in large part because of troubles in England, especially the collapse of Barings Bank. But Republicans saw another reason for the American disturbances in the outcome of the election. Senator John Sherman warned that once the Democrats took control of the House, "all sorts of financial schemes of the wildest character will be proposed, and, whatever may be the outcome, they will make capital timid." A full-scale panic was averted when the New York Clearing-House provided loan certificates to threatened banks, but unease continued to plague money and equity markets. Harrison took special care in preparing his second annual message, hoping to calm fears and buck up Republican spirits. "He is so deep in his message," wrote Mame Dimmick, "that we only see him at meals now, & he is not very talkative!!"[41]

Despite the Republicans' loss, they still held power in the second session of the previous Congress, and Harrison wanted nothing in his message that "savors of retreat." He congratulated the country on the first session's passage of "an unusual number of laws of very high importance." Although the effects of some were not yet fully realized, they promised greater prosperity and "better wages for our working people." The Anti-Lottery Law, the Dependent Pension Act, and the Meat Inspection Act were already demonstrating the wisdom of their passage. The increased currency resulting from the Silver Purchase Act had already exerted "a most beneficial influence upon business." With the recent money market stringency in mind, the president warned against any "impulsive legislation," that is, free coinage, that would threaten the nation's gold supply and monetary values.

Harrison also warned against any tinkering with the protective tariff, which was essential "to save our working people from the agitations and distresses" of "scant work and wages." The president decried the "misinformation" about high prices allegedly resulting from the tariff; the upward tendency of trade and commodity prices was the "natural and desired effect of the silver legislation" aimed at helping farmers. Reciprocity would also aid farmers, and Harrison defended the method he had written into the McKinley Act as a way to expedite beneficial trade agreements without the need to secure Senate approval. Since he had taken office, he declared, "the development of larger markets for our products, especially our farm products, has been kept constantly in mind, and no effort has been or will be spared to promote that end."

Harrison devoted the last quarter of his message to the bills still pending, most notably the elections bill. Federal election laws had been on the books for two decades, he observed, but the "present law stops just short of effectiveness, for it surrenders to the local authorities all control over the certification which establishes the *prima facie* right to a seat in the House of Representatives. This defect should be cured." He dismissed the Democrats' cry that this was a "force bill." Every law, whether national or state, "has force behind it; the courts, the marshal or constable, the *posse comitatus*, the prison, are all and always behind the law." Racial and sectional prejudice should not obscure the essential justice of the proposed reform: "The path of the elector to the ballot box must be free from the ambush of fear and the enticements of fraud; the count so true and open that none shall gainsay it."[42]

Harrison took heart that the overall impact of his message on congressional Republicans "seems to have been to brace them up." Even so, he wrote to Caroline, "I am a good deal troubled again over the silver question—but hope to be able to manage it." In early December, another severe monetary stringency led congressional silverites to push once again for free and unlimited coinage, a move that Harrison and his congressional allies were determined to forestall. To ease the currency shortage in the short term, the administration again ordered bond purchases and accelerated pension payments, and Harrison and Treasury Secretary Windom urged bankers to release funds from their own reserves. As a result, markets avoided an immediate crisis.[43]

Harrison and Windom also labored to meet the problem in the longer term. Working with a special committee of the Senate Republican caucus, they fashioned a legislative package for modest increases in silver purchases and national banknotes. In mid-December, John Sherman introduced the caucus bill, but shortly thereafter Nevada's William Stewart offered an amendment for free coinage. Since the session had opened, the Lodge elections bill had dominated Senate proceedings, with Democrats filibustering to prevent its passage. Now Stewart and other western silver Republicans were prepared to renounce their August pledge on the Lodge bill in order to curry favor with the Democrats in behalf of free coinage. In the words of Colorado's Edward Wolcott, "There are many things more important and vital to the welfare of this nation than that the colored citizens of the South shall vote."[44]

Harrison watched these developments with profound dismay. But, just as these issues came to the fore, the president was distracted by the horrific news of a bloody battle between army soldiers and Sioux Indians at Wounded Knee Creek in South Dakota. Harrison's policy toward Native Americans had closely followed the terms of the 1887 Dawes Severalty Act, which mandated the division of tribal lands into 160-acre allotments with the goal of putting each Indian, as Harrison said, "upon a farm" as "a self-supporting and responsible citizen." The program entailed the reversion of millions of acres to the U.S. government, and many Indians resisted the loss of their lands. Some, out of desperation, became adherents of the Ghost Dance, a cultish religion that promised the return of the buffalo and death to Indian enemies. In the fall of 1890, at the Pine Ridge Agency in South Dakota, the panicky and inexperienced Indian agent, who was a political hack recently appointed at the behest of the state's senator, began to send Washington overwrought warnings of imminent threats by Ghost Dancers to the agency and to white settlers. In response, Harrison ordered the military in the region to make preparations in case of an outbreak, but he questioned the wisdom of the agent's suggestion that the Ghost Dance leaders be arrested. Moreover, when he received reports that the Sioux were being cheated in land arrangements and were not receiving rations promised by the government, Harrison ordered the Interior Department to make a full investigation. In response, Thomas J. Morgan, commissioner of Indian affairs and a friend of

Harrison since Civil War days, presented a thirty-three-page report that described the government's dealings with the Indians but also attributed much of their resistance to an understandable discontent over the destruction of their way of life. "Those guilty of actual deeds of hostility should be punished," Morgan wrote, but "the great mass of them have a right to expect sympathy, help, and last, but by no means least, justice."[45]

While Harrison was studying Morgan's report, the news of Wounded Knee came in. Premeditated on neither side, the battle had erupted as soldiers of the Seventh Cavalry were attempting to disarm Indians in their control. It left twenty-five soldiers dead along with more than a hundred Indians, including many women and children. The president immediately demanded further information. To Nelson Miles, the general whose district included Wounded Knee, the War Department conveyed Harrison's direction that "if there was any unsoldierly conduct, you will relieve the responsible officer, and so use the troops engaged there as to avoid its repetition." Although hostile Indians remained in the area, the president suggested no attack but instead "watchful observation" in order to "give the Indians time to recover from their present excitement." Meanwhile, Harrison fired the Indian agent at Pine Ridge, and Miles suspended Colonel James W. Forsyth of the Seventh Cavalry, pending the investigation of his conduct. Despite Miles's low regard for Forsyth, the inquiry conducted by officers on Miles's staff essentially exonerated the colonel. Testimony suggested that while Forsyth's placement of his troops at the encounter had not been ideal, the killing of the women and children was due to their being intermingled among the Indian men. This account of the affair led officials in Washington, including Harrison, to reinstate Forsyth to his command.[46]

No new fighting erupted, and Harrison confessed to a friend his "great gratification" that the incident had "been closed so speedily, though the affair at Wounded Knee was a very bloody one." He started sketching out a special message to Congress but did not finish it, apparently deciding not to prolong discussion of the incident.

Of course, Harrison could not foresee the profound psychological impact that this last battle of the Indian Wars would have on both Indians and non-Indians in the ensuing decades. He made no fundamental change in administration policy. He did act to take the appointment of Indian agency medical personnel and educators out of the spoils system and place them under the civil service rules, a small but significant step toward improving services to the Native American population. Otherwise, he clung to the notion that "civilizing" the Native Americans was the key to a lasting solution to the Indian problem. He met with a delegation of Sioux leaders and urged them to give up war and take up the ways of virtuous citizenship. If they had complaints against agents or white settlers, they should register them "peacefully" with the government, which would do its best to protect them. Harrison advised the Indians to take their allotments of land "and endeavor the best you can to earn your living." "Every white man works for the bread and meat that sustains him," he declared, "and you must learn to do a little more for your own support every year."[47]

Some Democrats in Congress hoped to make political hay out of the Wounded Knee incident, but the Senate remained focused on the elections bill. Lodge had feared that the debate would be "only dress parade," and indeed the Democrats had been waging their filibuster against the bill for more than a month. Meanwhile, Harrison worked behind the scenes to bring the bill to a vote. "The President is anxious to take the responsibility if he is given the power," wrote a Republican congressman. "He feels deeply the humiliation, and I believe he would rather die trying to protect the rights of American citizens, than to live and not make the effort." Against the bill, Democrats counted on the help of western Republican silver senators. In the words of New Hampshire senator William Chandler, there was "no secret trade" between the two groups, but the "Democrats are so hostile to the Elections bill that they are about all willing to vote for free coinage in order to get the desired Republican votes against the Elections bill." On January 5, Stewart of Nevada made a surprise motion to take up the free coinage bill, which carried by a vote of 34 to 29, and the Lodge bill was thus laid aside. At least three Democrats who opposed free coinage nonetheless voted to take up Stewart's bill in order to block the elections bill. One, Arthur Gorman of Maryland, said that he "would have voted for the free coinage of lead" to block Lodge's bill.[48]

After little more than a week's debate, the Senate passed the silver bill. Still, the silverites had little hope of victory in the end. "Even should it pass the House," Nevada Republican senator John P. Jones wrote, "it is more than probable that the President would veto it." Indeed, the White House made clear Harrison's intention to block free coinage even if it were attached as a rider to an appropriations bill. Speaking for the administration, Windom told a New York audience that free coinage would be "extremely disastrous" to the American economy. In a tragic turn of events, Windom died immediately after the speech, and Harrison made certain that the selection of his successor signaled no change in policy. "I am in thorough accord with the President in his views of free coinage," the new Treasury secretary, Charles Foster, told reporters. While the bill languished in committee amid speculation about compromise, several House Republican leaders asked Harrison what they should do. "Nothing," he said. As one reporter put it, "It was this expression of will upon the part of the President that put an end absolutely to the silver agitation in Congress." The bill never came to a vote in the House.[49]

Directly after the Senate had passed the coinage bill, it voted to take up the elections bill once again, by a tie vote that required Vice President Levi Morton to tip the balance. The prospect of another filibuster loomed, and the bill's advocates moved to limit debate through cloture. But in a surprise move, Wolcott of Colorado made a motion to take up a pending apportionment bill and put aside the elections measure, which carried by one vote, 35 to 34. Four silver state Republicans plus two others voted with the Democrats. The Lodge bill was dead. Although Harrison had again begun to work behind the scenes for the bill, the effort failed. On this issue at least, as bill sponsor John Spooner put it, "The Confederacy and the Western mining camps are in legislative supremacy." Stewart defended the Republican silverites and charged that Harrison's "attempt to pass the Force bill through Congress aroused the whole country, and particularly the South, where the colored population was to be forced into power by a partisan President." Harrison saw the issue differently, and no one regretted the bill's demise more than he. "That the majority shall rule is an underlying principle of our institutions," he declared in a rare newspaper interview. "It will not do for the people of any section to say that they must be let alone, that it is a local question to be settled by the States of whether we shall have honest elections or not."[50]

Because the Democrats would control the next House, the prospect for election reform during the remainder of Harrison's term died with the adjournment of the Fifty-first Congress on March 3, 1891. As the months wore on, the "southern question" rapidly faded from American political discourse. On a tour through the South six weeks later, Harrison told an Atlanta audience that each American should "bravely and generously give every other man his equal rights before the law," but he saw little utility in reopening debate over the Lodge bill. Indeed, a few months later in a speech in Vermont, he acknowledged that "the prejudices of generations are not like marks upon the blackboard, that can be rubbed out with a sponge. These are more like the deep glacial lines that the years have left in the rock; but the water, when that surface is exposed to its quiet, gentle, and perpetual influence, wears even these out, until the surface is smooth and uniform."

When the new Congress convened in December 1891, Harrison gamely sought to revive the issue. Rather than calling for a reconsideration of the Lodge bill itself, however, he proposed that Congress create a bipartisan commission, to be appointed by the Supreme Court, to investigate ways of "securing to every elector a free and unmolested exercise of the suffrage." But even this modest proposal had no chance in the Democratic House. In this era, not only blacks' suffrage rights but their physical safety grew more precarious, and Harrison became the first president to attack lynchings. These perversions of justice, he said, "shame our Christian civilization." He called upon Congress to enact "the strongest repressive legislation" wherever the practice came under federal jurisdiction but again held no hope for action by the Democrats. And beyond Congress, Harrison's attempts at moral suasion on the issue had virtually no effect on the course of vigilante violence in the South. Still, even though Harrison failed to change white opinion, he won for himself a place of esteem among the nation's blacks. "To my mind," said Frederick Douglass, "we never had a greater President." Harrison's efforts for the elections bill "should endear him to the colored people as long as he lives."[51]

Despite the failure of the Lodge bill, the second session did add to the list of notable achievements of the Fifty-first Congress. Harrison had pushed two of these measures in particular. First, Congress passed a postal subsidy law whereby the government would pay steamship lines to carry overseas mail. As Harrison put it, these payments would "encourage the establishment of first-class steam communication" between American and foreign ports and thus foster the expansion of trade. Embracing government activism, he asserted that the public benefit fully justified the government "in making expenditures in the direction that no private enterprise could afford to go." Second, Harrison successfully pushed for a Forest Reserve Act, empowering the president to set aside public lands as national forests. In the course of his administration, he dedicated thirteen million acres as forest reserves.[52]

All told, the Fifty-first Congress passed 531 public laws, representing an unprecedented level of legislative accomplishment unequaled until Theodore Roosevelt's second term. After the final adjournment on March 3, the historian and Republican congressman Henry Cabot Lodge wrote, "No Congress in peace time since the first has passed so many great & important measures of lasting value to the people." Harrison agreed. "In many ways it has been a most remarkable Congress," he told an interviewer. "Its work has been of the most important character." The president had a right to be proud, for few of his predecessors had immersed themselves so thoroughly in the legislative process. As the *Indianapolis Journal* put it, Harrison had "higher views of the functions of administration than the beaten path of routine and precedent." But if the elections of 1890 were any indication, Harrison would not find it easy to translate this record of achievement into a successful bid for reelection.[53]

6

---

# Diplomacy and Defeat

The political configuration of the Fifty-second Congress offered President Harrison little prospect of achieving much on the legislative front except, perhaps, blocking mischief by the Democrats. Hence, in the second half of his term, Harrison devoted more of his time to foreign affairs. The administration settled into the traditional business of reacting to incidents, but it also labored to shape events to enhance the nation's standing and influence in the world. In this work, Harrison carried much of the load because of the continuing illnesses and absences of Secretary of State James G. Blaine. To his burdensome diplomatic labors, the president brought his seasoned mastery of detail and a lawyerly impulse to formulate an airtight case.

Harrison was also an indefatigable salesman for the administration's vision, as was clear from a tour he took across the country in the spring of 1891. In the final days of the Fifty-first Congress, the president found himself "worked and rushed to death" and was thus delighted at the prospect of a five-week trip through the South and out to the West Coast in April and May. He was accompanied by Caroline, who thought the five-car presidential special "the most beautiful train I ever saw, provided with every comfort & luxury." Also on board were Mary McKee, Russell Harrison and his wife, two cabinet officers, and several aides. Lizzie and John Parker had returned from Samoa, and in the spring Mame Dimmick had moved to their house in Washington. Mrs. Dimmick still remained a valued companion to the Harrisons, however, and they asked her to accompany them on their trip. Private secretary Elijah Halford stayed in Washington to keep the president informed of develop-ments there and elsewhere.[1]

Harrison traveled more than nine thousand miles through twenty-one states and two territories, making speeches to 140 audiences along the way. Included on the president's train were wire service reporters, and, as in the 1888 campaign, Harrison's words appeared in the newspapers that landed on citizens' breakfast tables every morning. He seized the opportunity to defend the activist policies of his administration. In his longest speech, given in Galveston, Texas, he pointed to the federally financed improvement of the city's harbor as a fine example of the "work which a liberal and united Government" could do. "This ministering care should extend to our whole country," he added. "We are great enough and rich enough to reach forward to grander conceptions than have entered the minds of some of our statesmen in the past." In Omaha, he spoke of his desire "by every method to enhance the prosperity of all our people; to have this great Government in all that it under-takes touch with beneficence and equal hands the pursuits of the rich and of the poor."

In San Francisco, Mrs. Harrison helped christen the new naval vessel *Monterey,* and the president underscored the central foreign policy theme that featured in many of his speeches: the administra-tion's focus on expanding the nation's trade. Harrison argued that reciprocity would open new ports to American products. The postal subsidy law would "put the American flag upon the seas" and give to "American bottoms a largely increased share of the com-merce of the world." The new navy would offer protection to those vessels as they headed for "the great distant marts and harbors of commerce." "I believe that we have come to a new epoch as a Nation," the president said in San Francisco. "There are opening portals before us inviting us to enter—opening portals to trade and influence and prestige such as we have never seen before." Buoyed by the "indescribable . . . cordiality of the people," Harrison returned to Washington "in a first rate condition of health" and ready to work.[2]

Even before the western trip, the work the president outlined in his speeches was well under way. The day after Harrison signed the McKinley Tariff, he and Blaine tapped Indiana Republican John W. Foster to conduct negotiations for reciprocity agreements. A seasoned diplomat, Foster had negotiated such pacts before and had served as an informal adviser to the administration during the preparation of the McKinley Act's reciprocity clause. He began work immediately. In early 1891 Foster struck his first deal with Brazil. Before leaving office, Harrison put into operation nine other agreements, mostly with Latin American states but with Austria-Hungary and Germany as well.[3]

Conspicuously missing from the list of reciprocal-trade partners was Canada, despite the Canadian government's ardent desire for an arrangement. Harrison and Blaine recognized that freer trade with the Canadian provinces would simply bring in more agricultural imports to compete with American farm products, while the Canadians would continue to buy manufactured goods from Great Britain rather than the United States. The whole point of tacking reciprocity on to the high tariff act was to appeal to farmers. Blaine thought that reciprocity could help the Republicans "break the [Farmers'] Alliance before six months," but an unprofitable reciprocity with Canada "would be one of the worst things among the farmers, in a political point of view, that we could do." Moreover, Blaine believed, high tariff barriers would eventually lead Canada to "seek admission to the Union." But the idea of "political union" with the country's northern neighbor had little appeal to Harrison, who told Blaine, "I am not much of an annexationist." He added, however, "I do feel that in some directions, as to naval stations and points of influence, we must look forward to a departure from the too conservative opinions which have been held heretofore."[4]

In any event, Harrison counted trade reciprocity as one of the chief diplomatic successes of his administration. In his last annual message, he reported that for countries with which the United States had made trade pacts, exports had risen by an average of more than 20 percent. But the experiment was short-lived; in 1894 the Democrats enacted a new tariff law that terminated the Harrison agreements.[5]

Soon after the passage of the postal subsidy act, the Post Office Department began to advertise for bids for ocean mail service. The law stimulated the development of only one new steamship company, but it also provided aid to existing lines. Before Harrison left office, the administration had signed eleven contracts for ocean mail service for payments totaling nearly a million dollars. Optimistically, Harrison estimated that the subsidies would result in forty-one mail steamers under the American flag, with a consequent enlargement of the carrying capacity of the American merchant fleet. Although the law had little impact in southern South America, it enhanced American traffic and commerce in the Caribbean region.[6]

One reason for the slow creation of contracts was the high standards applied to the construction and operation of qualifying ships. The law stipulated that the vessels should be "of the highest rating known to maritime commerce" and so constructed as to allow for "prompt and economical conversion into auxiliary naval cruisers." In essence, the mail steamers would constitute a U.S. naval reserve. The ships could be "taken and used by the United States" for a payment of fair value to the owners and, if needed, these carriers of commerce could be pressed into service as defenders of commerce or other national interests. But Harrison did not regard such a reserve naval fleet as anything more than a potential supplement to the real thing. Appropriations for and construction of the new navy continued under full steam, so that by the close of Harrison's term, the navy had launched twenty-five new vessels.[7]

Concerns for the mobility of the new navy gave added impetus to the long-standing interest in a prospective canal through Central

America, which Harrison considered of "transcendent importance to the commerce of this country, and, indeed, to the commercial interests of the world." Congress had granted a charter to a private concern, the Maritime Canal Company, which won a concession from Nicaragua and began construction in 1889. Harrison reported regularly to Congress on the company's progress, but the undertaking was too vast to depend solely on private investment. In his third annual message, delivered in December 1891, the president told Congress that he was "quite willing" to recommend financing of the project "by direct appropriations from the Treasury." Such a proposal had scant chance of winning approval, however, and Harrison threw his support behind a bill to have the government guarantee the company's bonds. He readily crossed party lines and worked closely with the bill's most ardent sponsor, Alabama Democratic senator John T. Morgan. Unfortunately, there was bipartisan opposition to the bill as well; some in Congress regarded the loan guarantee as unconstitutional, while others considered the construction project itself unfeasible and wasteful. The bill failed to reach a vote before Harrison's term expired.[8]

The prospect of a trans-isthmian canal heightened support in Washington for the acquisition of bases that would enable the navy to safeguard approaches to the waterway as well as defend other American interests. In his inaugural address, Harrison had called attention to the navy's need for "convenient coaling stations," although he insisted that the country should obtain them "only by means that do not in any degree partake of coercion." Among the desirable sites for such bases was the Môle St. Nicholas in Haiti.

The administration initially entrusted negotiations for a base at the Môle to the American minister in Haiti, the prominent black leader Frederick Douglass. Douglass proceeded cautiously, believing, as he later stated, that Harrison did not want him to "press the matter" to the point where a forced concession by the Haitian government would arouse revolution against it at home. But other officials in Washington, especially navy secretary Benjamin Tracy, who had close ties with New York businessmen holding commercial interests in Haiti, considered Douglass's approach too timid. Harrison consented to the assignment of a naval officer, Rear Admiral Bancroft Gherardi, as a special commissioner to assist Douglass. The admiral's arrival in Haiti with a fleet of five ships, soon joined by four others, triggered just the opposite of its intended effect. In meetings with the Haitian foreign minister, Gherardi dominated the discussions and, with a combination of arrogance and intimidation, undid whatever goodwill Douglass had created for the project. When the envoys reported their lack of progress, Harrison refused to sanction the use of force. The Haitians dug in their heels and refused even the lease of a base.[9]

While the Haitian negotiations were nearing their fruitless end, the dictator of Haiti's nearly bankrupt neighbor, the Dominican Republic, approached American officials about the possible lease of Samaná Bay for an American base. The ensuing talks proceeded with some success, but the refinancing of the Dominican debt by a syndicate of American bankers led the Dominicans to change their mind, and the lease deal fell through. The American minister to Denmark raised the possibility of pushing for the annexation of the Danish West Indies, but the administration considered these islands of minimal commercial or strategic value and a burden to defend in case of war. In the end, Harrison established no naval base in the Caribbean.[10]

As Harrison's reaction to the Danish West Indies question demonstrated, his overseas ambitions were neither boundless nor haphazard but, instead, targeted to do the country the most good. In the summer of 1891, Portugal sent an emissary to meet the American minister in Paris, Whitelaw Reid, to suggest the establishment of American bases in Portugal's African colonies, in the Azores, or even in Lisbon. Harrison emphatically said no. "Either a sole or joint military occupancy of ports either in Portugal or in Africa . . . would be so flagrant a departure from the settled and traditional policy of this Government & it would involve so much risk of foreign embroilment that it is not to be thought of." Harrison further explained to Reid, "I did not feel that it was very important for us to secure coaling stations for our men of war in either the European or African possessions of Portugal, but have regarded it as very important that in the West Indies, in the Pacific Islands, South America &c, we should have such stations. It seems quite unlikely that we shall be called upon to conduct naval warfare except on or near the shores of this hemisphere."

Blaine agreed. He regarded the Portuguese offer as "entirely inadmissable." In his view, he told the president, "there are only three places that are of value enough to be taken, that are not continental. One is Hawaii and the others are Cuba and Porto Rico." But he noted that the two Caribbean islands "are not now imminent and will not be for a generation." Somewhat cryptically he added, "Hawaii may come up for decision at any unexpected hour and I hope we shall be prepared to decide it in the affirmative."[11]

Blaine had sent as the American minister to Hawaii his Maine friend John L. Stevens, who steadily fed the secretary reports of the American-descended sugar planters' dissatisfaction with the native government. Discontent in the islands increased after the passage of the McKinley Tariff, whose free-sugar provision undermined the advantage in sugar exports that Hawaii had enjoyed under a reciprocity treaty signed in 1887. To help ease the islands' economic woes, the Hawaiian government pushed for a new treaty that would institute full free trade between the two countries. Harrison did not rush to embrace this proposition. In the fall of 1891, he told Blaine that "the necessity of maintaining and increasing our hold and influence in the Sandwich Islands is very apparent and very pressing," but he had not resolved "how far we can go in extending our trade relations." Although Blaine proceeded with talks with Hawaii's representatives, Harrison never approved the treaty that the secretary achieved. He thought the pact had scant chance of passing in the Senate, where many Republicans would regard even this limited version of free trade as inconsistent with the GOP's protectionist philosophy. With an election year looming, the president hesitated to reignite the tariff controversy sparked by the McKinley Act. In his last annual message, given in December 1892, Harrison ignored the Hawaiian free-trade proposal. To enhance trade with the islands, he favored the laying of a telegraph cable under the Pacific and the development of a harbor and base at Pearl River, the concession for which had been granted in the 1887 treaty.[12]

In his last message, Harrison noted that exports had reached the unprecedented level of one billion dollars, an increase of more than one-third above the average of exports for the previous ten years. The nation also enjoyed a favorable balance of trade, exports exceeding imports by more than two hundred million dollars. Despite the failure of some administration initiatives, Harrison was convinced of the overall success of his broad-gauged policy of economic expansion. Moreover, the resolute assertion of American power that characterized Harrison's economic foreign policies carried over into the more traditional work of dealing with incidents and disputes that arose. Here, as well, Harrison demanded that other countries accord the United States the respect and treatment due a first-class power. In the words of one scholar, Harrison was helping to usher in a "new paradigm" in America's foreign relations.[13]

This new assertiveness was apparent in an imbroglio that marred usually friendly relations with Italy in the spring of 1891. In March a New Orleans jury acquitted several Mafia-connected Italians accused of killing the city's police chief. Allegations of jury intimidation abounded, and a frustrated mob proceeded, with little hindrance from the local police, to lynch eleven Italians held in custody: three Italian subjects and eight naturalized Italian Americans. The Italian government registered a fervent protest and demanded that the responsible parties be brought to justice. Blaine explained that federalism left the national government no power in the case, but he and Harrison did urge the governor of Louisiana to act to prevent further violence and to bring the perpetrators to justice.

The Italian government, confronting a vocal opposition at home, refused to accept the administration's explanation and expression of regret, and withdrew its minister from Washington. Uncowed, Harrison called home the American minister, who happened to be his former law partner Albert G. Porter. In order to save face at home, the Italian government insisted upon an indemnity. The administration thought such a payment possible, but, with Blaine's full backing, Harrison adamantly refused to negotiate until Rome sent its minister back to the United States. "You know I have been very decided in my views about this case from the beginning," the president wrote Blaine. "They acted hastily & foolishly & ought not to have too much help in a necessary retreat." There the matter stalled for nearly a year. Significantly, Harrison did not allow the dispute to interfere with American pressure on Italy to lift its ban on the import of American meat products (which it did in October 1891). Finally, in the spring of 1892, the affair ended amicably when the two countries agreed to return their respective ministers to duty simultaneously and the United States agreed in principle to pay an indemnity.[14]

While the Italian dispute simmered, another incident sparked a vigorous response from Harrison and initiated a crisis that could easily have ended in war. In mid-October 1891, American sailors on shore leave from the USS *Baltimore* in Valparaiso, Chile, found themselves in a far-flung fight with local Chileans, which left two Americans dead, more than a dozen wounded, and three dozen arrested. Chilean authorities claimed that the fray grew out of a barroom quarrel; Americans in Chile and in Washington saw it as a violent act of resentment against the United States for its alleged tilt of support for the losing faction during the recent civil war in Chile. The captain of the *Baltimore* reported to Washington that an investigation conducted by several of his officers found that the American sailors had been unarmed and that some of their wounds had resulted from bayonet thrusts, indicating participation by the police in the attack.[15]

With Blaine still not back from Bar Harbor, Harrison took immediate personal charge of the American response. He drafted a strongly worded message to Chile, which was sent over the signature of Assistant Secretary of State William Wharton. The president demanded to know if the Chileans could offer "any explanation" of the mob's "cruel work," which he characterized as "an apparent expression of unfriendliness" toward the United States. When after several weeks he received no satisfactory reply, Harrison turned up the heat in his annual message to Congress. He described the street fight as an act of "hostility to those men as sailors of the United States, wearing the uniform of their Government." The United States, he declared, would "expect full and prompt reparation." At the same time, the navy began discreet preparations for war.[16]

A few days later, the Chilean minister of foreign affairs, Manuel Antonio Matta, inflamed the situation by declaring that Harrison had based his message on "erroneous or deliberately incorrect" statements. Regarding the *Baltimore* incident, Matta said, there was "no exactness nor sincerity in what is said at Washington." Moreover, a Chilean criminal investigation continued to treat the case as one simply of a brawl of drunken sailors, both Chilean and American. The Chilean government did express its sincere regret— "sentimiento muy sincero"—concerning the episode, but State Department translators, responding to a query from the president, concluded that in using the phrase, the Chileans offered merely their regret that it had occurred rather than contrition for Chileans' having caused it. The navy escalated its preparations for war, and Harrison met with the Democratic chairman of the House Committee on Foreign Affairs, who assured him that whenever he decided to lay the question before Congress, it would be "treated outside of any partisan feelings."[17]

With dim prospect for a satisfactory solution, Harrison convened a cabinet meeting to frame a response. Blaine, who in the interest of his trade initiatives had tried to soften the U.S. position, took ill and left the meeting. Harrison proceeded to draft a note to Chile demanding "adequate reparation for the injury done" to the United States. He denounced Matta's December statement as "in the highest degree offensive" and threatened to terminate diplomatic relations unless Chile withdrew it with a "suitable apology." When the president received no immediate response, he sent Congress a double-barrelled special message. The message was not unlike the legal briefs Harrison had written as a lawyer—only this time the case was in the court of national and world opinion. He carefully recounted the Valparaiso incident and its diplomatic aftermath and insisted that it was unacceptable for Chile to use "words of small or equivocal meaning" in offering "an apology for an offense so atrocious as this." The president consigned the matter to Congress, whose power to declare war he respected, "for such action as may be deemed necessary."[18]

The affair ended anticlimactically when the Chileans capitulated completely to Harrison's demands. They agreed to a reparation for the dead and wounded sailors and withdrew the offensive portions of Matta's dispatch, which, they said, had been employed "through an error of judgment." Harrison was satisfied. Although Blaine engaged in a bit of private bluster with friends that he would resign if Harrison did not accept Chile's apology, there was never any doubt that the president would accept. Indeed, he and Blaine vied with each other to find the most cordial words to express America's renewed goodwill for their Latin neighbor. Several months later, the Chileans paid a seventy-five-thousand-dollar indemnity.[19]

Harrison also employed his lawyer's skills and a bit of timely saber rattling in dealing with the most serious and persistent issue that his administration confronted with Great Britain, the nettlesome question of the hunting of fur seals in the Bering Sea. The home base of the seals was the Pribilof Islands, which were part of Alaska, although the animals might swim hundreds of miles out into the Bering in search of food. American law forbade taking seals in the open water—pelagic sealing—and an American firm, the North American Commercial Company, enjoyed a monopoly of limited hunting on the islands. The chief violators of the ban on pelagic sealing were Canadian sealers, although the law had not been enforced until the first Cleveland administration, when the United States seized several Canadian vessels. Just before Harrison succeeded Cleveland, Congress passed a law directing the president to issue annual warnings that the United States would arrest pelagic sealers. The American policy rested on a claim that the United States had a property right in the seals wherever they were because their principal rookeries were on American soil. The British, who still handled foreign relations for Canada, maintained that the United States had no legal right to ban sealing in international waters.

Harrison issued the required warning soon after taking office and again in 1890, but enforcement by American revenue cutters was distinctly unaggressive. What Harrison desired was not a policing operation that could invite military reprisal from Britain but instead a permanent agreement between the two countries that would avert conflict and preserve the seal herd. Preliminary discussions of a possible arbitration began in mid-1890. Because Harrison saw the dispute as essentially a legal issue, he played the leading role in formulating and sustaining the American position. In mid-December he framed the key questions to be submitted to arbitration: What jurisdictional rights had Russia claimed in the Bering Sea when it owned Alaska? How far had Britain conceded those claims? Did Russia's rights pass to the United States when it acquired Alaska? Did the United States have any property right in the seals when they ventured beyond the three-mile limit? And what regulations might be necessary to preserve the herd? Harrison wrote at the bottom of his draft: "Mr. Blaine, after reading this twice said, It is splendid—not the slightest change is necessary." Within two months, Britain accepted this proposal as the basis for an arbitration, although it required another year of tedious negotiations to work out an acceptable clause relating to damages for the American seizure of Canadian ships. The clause assigned arbitrators the task of determining the facts but not the monetary liability. Again Harrison's wording prevailed in the final treaty, which was signed on February 29, 1892. (The arbitration, held in Paris after Harrison's term, decided against the United States on all major points.)[20]

While an arbitration could conclusively settle the underlying issues, Harrison confronted the matter of protecting the seal herd in the short term. Negotiations for a modus vivendi prohibiting sealing began in the spring of 1891. The Canadians urged the British to resist such an agreement, while Harrison came under similar importunity from the American fur seal company, whose leaders numbered some influential Republican party leaders. Despite this pressure, Blaine told Harrison that it would be a "serious political mistake to allow contractors full liberty with seals, and refuse co-operations with England in rigidly preserving all seals for this year." The president agreed that "on the whole it is best [to] stop killing this season." Thus, by mid-June, Harrison and the British agreed to prohibit all pelagic sealing and to limit the island catch of the company to 7,500. This modus would last until May 1, 1892. In Halford's words, the modus was "a great triumph and the President felt very good over it."[21]

The next year, as the arbitration treaty was nearing completion, it seemed only natural to renew the modus vivendi, but the British, upon insistence by the Canadians, refused. Instead, Lord Salisbury, the British prime minister, suggested a new modus permitting pelagic sealing thirty miles beyond land and allowing a land catch of up to thirty thousand. Harrison flatly rejected it. The British proposal put in jeopardy the very property whose status the two parties had agreed to submit to arbitration. When Salisbury again refused to extend the existing agreement, Harrison replied that the United States would have no choice but to defend its property rights unilaterally—which, he implied, could lead to an armed clash in the Bering Sea. Moreover, he warned the British, if they insisted on unfettered pelagic sealing, the question for the United States would be "no longer one of pecuniary loss or gain, but one of honor and self-respect." Blaine, ailing once again, had written Harrison to warn that "get[ting] up a war cry" would raise political dangers and intensify the conflict with Britain as well. Nonetheless, Harrison stuck to his course. He went to Blaine's house to show him the draft of his latest insistent note to Britain, and the secretary saw no choice but to pronounce it "first rate." The tension in Washington over the issue was such that one of the president's aides who helped prepare the note wrote in his journal that "the outcome means a backdown on [the] part of G.B. or war." But Harrison was taking a risk that was more calculated than reckless: He had acquired through back channels reliable information that the British would not go to war over sealing. His gamble paid off. Although the British minister, Julian Pauncefote, referred to Harrison as "that obstinate and pugnacious little President," he followed Salisbury's orders and backed down. The previously skittish Blaine now wrote Harrison, "It is as I thought with Lord Salisbury! He will agree to your last proposal." In early April 1892, Blaine and Pauncefote signed a renewed modus vivendi almost identical to the first one. Once again, Harrison's tenacious personal diplomacy paid off.[22]

At the outset of the Bering Sea negotiations in the spring of 1891, while Harrison was on his speaking trip in California, Blaine wired the president that it was "embarrassing . . . not to have [the] advantage of your presence." Harrison offered to cut short his trip if necessary, but Blaine's comment must have rankled, coming as it did from a key figure in the cabinet who refused to forgo his long summer vacations in Maine. In May, before Harrison returned to Washington, Blaine suffered a physical collapse while visiting Andrew Carnegie in New York. His condition remained precarious for several days, after which he went to Bar Harbor for a convalescence that lasted until late October. Harrison immediately telegraphed the secretary his "great regret and much concern" over his sickness, but the president could not have relished Mrs. Blaine's comment to a reporter: "Since the President's absence from Washington Mr. Blaine has been working very hard, and, the fact is that he was called upon to look after all the affairs of the Department of State."

Harrison may not have considered it out of line to expect Blaine to manage his own department, but in fact the president shouldered much of the burden even when Blaine was in Washington and much more when he was away, especially during the secretary's long absence in 1891. Harrison was not always convinced that either Blaine or the country appreciated what he was doing. He generally kept his irritation under wraps, but Caroline was less discreet with family members. "Your Father has been very busy with the Bering Sea matter," she wrote to daughter Mary McKee. "Mr. Blaine has not yet been well enough to give any attention to it, yet the papers are trying to make out that B— did it all." In mid-June, when negotiations with Spain for reciprocity with Cuba and Puerto Rico were concluded, the president thought it would be a gracious gesture to send the papers to Maine for Blaine's signature, but the messenger reported that Blaine signed off perfunctorily. "I am rather disgusted with the way he & his friends act in the matter," Caroline wrote Mary McKee.

> They claim all the credit when your Father has done all the work. Your Father thought it a courteous thing to send the papers prepared under his care to Mr. B. to read. Mrs. B. wrote that he was unable to read them. Blaine is a genius but he is not a *manly man* by any means. Such conduct as your Father has shown him would make a noble disposition speak out.

Harrison felt the sting and was glad when his foreign policy adviser, John W. Foster, and some other party leaders began to give press interviews "giving me credit for having the directing hand even in diplomatic matters." "Don't give yourself any worry," he told Caroline in September, perhaps with more hope than conviction, "from now on you will see that my labors & real relations to this administration will be better appreciated. This—not a renomination—is all either of us has cared for."[23]

Caroline Harrison may not have cared for another term in what she described as "this *troublesome* position," but the president's attitude was more complicated. Certainly he considered the labors of his office "exacting and troublesome," much of it even "drudgery." After two and a half years, he found himself "very much worn out." But he did desire some stamp of approval from the American people, and the surest kind of endorsement was renomination and reelection. Harrison did not withdraw his name from consideration, which he could have done had he truly wished to step down, but neither did he consider it proper to make a public announcement that he wanted to run again in 1892. He seemed to harbor the notion that Republicans ought to assume that his successful administration merited his reelection and that a renomination should be his to refuse. But seasoned political organizers eventually recognized that the president could not simply drift into a renomination. As early as midsummer 1891, Louis Michener, who had engineered Harrison's nomination in 1888, told private secretary Elijah Halford that he was "anxious for the day when a charge will be ordered all along the line."[24]

Michener's eagerness to launch an aggressive effort in Harrison's behalf was in response to a growing movement within the party against his renomination. At the core of that movement were party leaders such as Thomas Platt of New York and Matthew Quay of Pennsylvania, who still remained alienated because of Harrison's treatment of them over patronage matters. These men threw their support to Blaine, the only Republican with sufficient stature and popularity to mount a realistic challenge to the president. But whether the ailing secretary would agree to the use of his name against his chief remained problematic. In late July 1891 A. L. Conger, national Republican committeeman from Ohio and a Blaine supporter, reported to a secret meeting of the party's executive committee in Washington that Blaine had told him he would not be an open candidate but would accept if, as Michener reported to Halford, "the convention saw fit to tender the nomination in such a way as to make it complimentary, and show the nomination to be in accord with the wishes of the party." Michener warned that the Blaine supporters would claim that "perfect harmony" existed between Harrison and Blaine and that the president would give way to the secretary, "and in this way they will try to strengthen themselves with the people." It was time for Harrison's camp to act to combat this scheme.[25]

In the remaining months of 1891, Michener, working closely with Halford, began to coordinate the push for Harrison, especially in Indiana. There former congressman Stanton J. Peele pursued a quiet organizing effort. The chief objection to the president among some disgruntled Hoosier Republicans, Peele told Michener, was simply that "he has appointed Tom instead of John," while "the business men, the manufacturers and farmers of this state are with the administration." The key, he believed, was "to get the manufacturers and business men aroused when the time comes to attend the primaries [local conventions], and to that end I shall work." Harrison himself maintained his nondeclared status, but in late August he took an extended speaking tour through Vermont and New York, emphasizing the nation's prosperity wrought by his administration's policies. "The President's fine speeches on his trip," Michener wrote Halford, "are pleasing his friends greatly, and doing him much good."[26]

Harrison and his allies also tried to build bridges to their antagonists. In late July Quay resigned as Republican national chairman, and Harrison accepted as his replacement James S. Clarkson, despite the Iowan's rumored leaning toward Blaine. In a conference with Michener, Clarkson reported that Blaine was "feeling kindly enough" toward the president but that his family was still "quite bitter" over Harrison's refusal to appoint Walker Blaine assistant secretary of state. "The family talk is of such a character as to be very prejudicial, and there is no telling how soon it may drive [Blaine] to take a stand which he would otherwise not think of." As for Clarkson's attitude, Michener wrote Halford, "While he cannot be said to be in love with the President, neither is he in love with the other man." What he wanted was acknowledgment of his party leadership and organizational work. At Michener's urging, Harrison invited Clarkson and the new national vice chairman, Garrett Hobart, to dine at the White House, where they discussed at length the condition of the party. The next day Harrison wrote to Caroline in Cape May that as far as political matters were concerned, "You can rest assured that they are improving every day." Within the week, Harrison asked Clarkson's opinion about Iowa men he was considering for appointment to the Interstate Commerce Commission, and Clarkson responded in a warm letter commending the president's "remarkable ability in searching the whole field." In addition, when Secretary of War Redfield Proctor resigned, Harrison seized the opportunity to make another gesture toward reconciliation by appointing Stephen B. Elkins, long known as a Blaine man.[27]

Harrison's supporters championed the president at Republican conventions in the handful of states holding elections in 1891. Republican platforms in Iowa, Massachusetts, Ohio, and New York all praised the administration and the president by name; some also commended the administration's foreign policy without mentioning Blaine's name. The Pennsylvania convention "heartily" endorsed the Harrison administration but rejected a plank sponsored by Quay's minions calling for Blaine's nomination in 1892. Instead, the Keystone State party saluted Blaine for his "brilliant administration of the State Department."[28]

These successes by the president's supporters did not completely derail the anti-Harrison movement, and the pressure mounted on Blaine to step forward as its avowed leader. For their part, the Harrison men did not relax but drove their cause even harder. A key test of strength occurred in Indiana in January 1892 in the elections of members of the Republican state committee. In Indiana, friends of Harrison's old rival Walter Q. Gresham had joined the Blaine men in opposition to the president. Nonetheless, Peele and his allies dominated the district conventions and secured the selection of a solid Harrison committee and endorsements of his renomination by all but one of the thirteen district meetings. After this triumph, Peele reported to Halford that nearly all prominent men in the state who had opposed Harrison were "now friendly to the administration and favor renomination. . . . You see it is a good thing to lick a fellow once in a while." Harrison was pleased by his supporters' efforts. "A renomination for the Presidency is a thing I could very well forego," he wrote to one. "Indeed I think my comfort and health and personal interests would all be subserved by that course. I feel, however, in the present aspect of affairs, that it would have been disappointing if the Indiana Republicans had shown indifference in view of the organized attack that has been attempted."[29]

This action in Indiana demonstrated that Blaine, however popular he might be, could not expect the party's nomination without a terrific fight. The secretary dreaded not only that sort of intra-party warfare but an arduous fall campaign as well, and he was not even sure that he was equal to the rigors of the presidency. Two weeks after the committee elections in Indiana, Blaine announced in a published letter to Clarkson that he was not a candidate and that his name would not go before the national convention in Minneapolis. He did not, however, endorse the president, thereby leaving open the possibility that he would accept a draft or throw his support to someone else.

Treasury secretary Charles Foster told the president that even though the letter was "not all that could reasonably be expected," Harrison should be "cordial and gracious" about it to Blaine. In fact, however, their relations deteriorated even more during the spring. Foreign policy crises were brewing with Italy, Chile, and Great Britain, yet the two men conferred almost exclusively by correspondence, and at times their letters showed distinct testiness. In addition, in March Blaine requested that Harrison promote his son-in-law, John Coppinger, a colonel in the army, to brigadier general. When Harrison said that he could not jump Coppinger over more than fifty other colonels who had more seniority, Blaine accepted the explanation, but Mrs. Blaine did not. She confronted Harrison, as he put it, with "fierce words" and "a harsh look on her face," but he was unmoved. Temperatures rose even higher in early May when a Democratic newspaper in New York published a report that Harrison's son, Russell, had been saying that the idea of nominating Blaine was "absurd" because the secretary was "completely broken down both mentally and physically." Both Harrison and Russell denied the story, but the Blaines neither forgave nor forgot.[30]

Meanwhile, the selection of national convention delegates proceeded in the states. Harrison took greatest pleasure that Indiana chose a solid delegation in his favor. He thanked the Hoosier state chairman, John Gowdy, but he also thought that "the work should go right on," especially the compiling of "as large a list as possible" of voters to receive political literature. In addition, he told Gowdy, he would "be glad to cooperate with you in smoothing out any misunderstandings." Other states chose Harrison delegates as well, although sometimes the state conventions forbore passing specific instructions for Harrison in order to avoid unseemly rows with his opponents.[31]

Still, despite Blaine's February withdrawal, Platt, Quay, and some other party leaders remained disaffected. Fearful that Platt would knife Harrison in the fall, some of the president's advisers urged him to meet the boss to mend fences, but he saw such a meeting as useless. "I do not know of any offense that I have given that it is possible for me to repair," Harrison told one New York ally. "You know that I cannot promise anything to anybody and that I will not so talk as to let people think I am making promises." As for his campaign in general, with less than a month to go before the convention and with Blaine supposedly out of the race, Harrison believed he could maintain his behind-the-scenes role, telling one friend, "I have not felt that it was appropriate in me to press myself in any way upon the party."[32]

But was Blaine out of the race? In late May several antiadministration leaders met in Detroit and concluded that Blaine's withdrawal was not final and that he would accept a nomination. A few days later, Blaine himself went to New York City where, according to one newspaper, he "put himself ostentatiously on exhibition" to show "that he was in good health and spirits." More important, Blaine discussed his prospects in a closed-door meeting with Platt, who said that for the secretary to back out now would be unfair to the men who had worked for him.[33]

The Detroit meeting and Blaine's New York trip, both splashed in the newspapers, convinced Harrison that it was time to remove the gloves. To take charge of his campaign, he called in Louis Michener, telling his old manager, "No Harrison has ever retreated in the presence of a foe without giving battle." With barely two weeks before the Republicans were to convene in Minneapolis, Michener zealously set to work. "The President," Halford wrote, "seems to be pleased with the fact that his friends are cutting loose." Michener arranged pro-Harrison statements by leading party figures and convinced many to go to Minneapolis to lobby delegates directly. To raise a fund for convention expenses for his team of workers, he dunned cabinet members for five hundred dollars each, although one, not surprisingly, did not contribute. Michener and his allies arrived in Minneapolis and opened the Harrison headquarters on June 1, a full week before the convention started. As each state delegation arrived in town, one of Michener's aides became its constant companion and watchdog.[34]

While the contest heated up in Minneapolis, Blaine sent his resignation to Harrison on June 4, and the president accepted it immediately. The previous July, members of the national committee had told a Blaine representative that if the secretary desired the presidential nomination, he would have to resign or brand himself as a dishonorable man. Now, after vacillating for nearly a year, he took the fateful step. Many believed that the ailing secretary had finally given in to the importunities of men such as Platt and Quay as well as those of his wife, whose hatred for the president had become well known. "Well, the crisis has come," Harrison told Halford. Mame Dimmick, who was at the White House, recorded in her diary that Blaine had "proved himself a traitor to the President." At Harrison's behest, Halford wired Michener and others in Minneapolis urging "care and caution."[35]

The news of Blaine's resignation energized both camps in Minneapolis, where the convention opened on June 7. But Blaine's act gave pause to some men, those more anti-Harrison than pro-Blaine, who feared that the charge of treachery would put Blaine on the defensive if he were nominated. Some cast about for an alternative candidate, and among the names heard most commonly was that of William McKinley, who had won election as Ohio's governor in 1891. In a master stroke, Michener and his allies accepted a move to make McKinley permanent chairman of the convention, believing that he could not well preside over any effort to stampede the convention to himself.[36]

Harrison's managers were confident that they had a majority of the delegates, but they feared that if the voting went beyond a single ballot, some of their delegates might wander to other candidates. Thus, they considered it imperative to achieve a vote of their full strength—and victory—on the first ballot. The day before the voting was to occur, the managers quietly assembled a caucus of all the delegates known to be for Harrison, but without telling them the purpose of the meeting. When the group had assembled in Market Hall, Michener and his allies transformed it into a rally for Harrison as a way of confirming delegates' commitments and demonstrating the inevitability of the president's renomination. New Yorker Chauncey Depew presided and declared that the Harrison men hoped "by the power of gravitation, by which larger bodies always attract smaller ones, to draw to us those of our opponent brethren who may want to come into the fold of the blessed." A formal roll call revealed that a majority of all the delegates was present and prepared to stand by Harrison. This Market Hall meeting practically settled the contest. At the White House, Harrison played with his grandchildren and, according to an aide, received news of the meeting with a demeanor "as cool & self possessed as if it was a democratic convention."[37]

The formal count came the next day. On June 10 the delegates heard nominating speeches for Harrison and Blaine and then proceeded directly to a vote. With 453 votes necessary for a choice, Harrison prevailed with 535⅙ to 182⅙ for Blaine and 182 for McKinley. Of the forty-four states, Harrison received some votes from forty. He received the solid vote of Indiana and five other states, and a majority from twenty others. Blaine received support from thirty states, a unanimous vote from four, and a majority in two others. Twenty-five states gave votes to McKinley. Platt managed to secure thirty-five New York votes for Blaine to twenty-seven for Harrison and ten for McKinley. Quay's Pennsylvania delegates cast forty-two votes for McKinley, nineteen for Harrison, and three for Blaine. When Ohio was called, forty-five delegates voted for McKinley, and McKinley cast the state's lone vote for Harrison, in what the president labeled "a clear pretense." "No mature man can believe," Harrison later wrote, "that Ohio voted for him without his consent . . . nor that the Governor of Ohio and the head of the Ohio delegation could influence no single vote therein, save his own." Harrison never forgave McKinley. Later in the evening, the convention honored New York's suggestion and by acclamation gave the vice presidential nomination to Whitelaw Reid, owner of the *New York Tribune*, former minister to France, and a longtime supporter of Blaine.[38]

At the White House, Mame Dimmick wrote that there was "great rejoicing at the glorious victory" after "a warm contest against trickery and disloyalty." In a rare self-revelatory comment, Harrison himself confessed that he felt "personal gratification" at the result. "I saw the organization against me, did not underrate its force, and knew also how it could have been placated; but I deliberately made up my mind that come what might at Minneapolis there would be found no dust on my knees when it was over." Still, more detached observers harbored fears that the victory might indeed turn out to be Pyrrhic. As one of the president's convention managers wrote to Halford, "The fact remains that there exists a deep sense of personal humiliation on the part of gentlemen who felt that their combined efforts could accomplish anything in political circles in this country."[39]

A renomination by a vote of less than 60 percent of the national convention proved hardly a solid base for an incumbent president to launch a campaign for reelection. At the Democratic convention two weeks later, by contrast, Grover Cleveland easily beat back a minor challenge to his third presidential nomination and retained command of his party in what was beginning to look like a Democratic year.[40]

In the weeks following the Republican convention, Harrison moved to repair fissures within the party. To replace Blaine as secretary of state, he turned to Chauncey Depew, who had long been a conciliator among Republican factions in New York. Depew declined, however, arguing that he could be more useful on the stump. More important, Depew told the president that because of his position as head of the New York Central Railroad, his entering the cabinet would likely alienate farmers whom Harrison was trying to woo. Harrison then tapped John W. Foster, who had backed Harrison's Indiana rival, Walter Gresham, in 1888, and who had in recent years performed considerable service in various State Department negotiations. (Foster's grandson John Foster Dulles was secretary of state in the 1950s.) As for nonessential appointments, Harrison took Reid's advice to defer them until after the election to avoid making new enemies.[41]

Harrison also sought a reorganization of the party's national committee. Clarkson's action against the president in the convention compelled his stepping down as chairman, although he retained a seat on the executive committee and worked in the campaign. Several men whom Harrison approached declined the chairmanship, which finally went to Thomas H. Carter of Montana, a former congressman who held a position in the administration as commissioner of the General Land Office. Harrison hoped that Carter's backing of free coinage of silver would help attract support in the West. But even though Harrison thought that the thirty-seven-year-old Carter was "a very bright, judicious, level-headed fellow . . . and thoroughly loyal," he was an amateur compared to Clarkson or the 1888 chairman, Matthew Quay.[42]

Harrison was more than willing "to do my part" in the campaign, but the serious illness of Caroline Harrison drew increasingly upon his time, attention, and spirit. During her years in the White House, Mrs. Harrison frequently suffered from respiratory ailments that some outsiders attributed to her spending too much time in the mansion's clammy basement and dusty attic while she pursued her renovation efforts. She was stricken again in April 1892. For months, Harrison ascribed her malady to nervous exhaustion, but he grew increasingly anxious when she showed no sustained recovery. Her doctors forbade her usual summer sojourn at the Jersey shore, and in early July Harrison took her to a cottage near Loon Lake, New York, where he hoped that "a summer in the Adirondacks will give her perfect health again." Because Congress would not adjourn for another month, Harrison returned to Washington and left Carrie in the care of her doctor and Mame Dimmick, who were soon joined by a trained nurse. From Washington, where filibusterers droned on in the House, Harrison wrote daughter Mary McKee, "Politics & business have been crowding me day & night & this with the anxiety about your mother makes life just now a burden & ambition a delusion."[43]

Congress adjourned on the evening of August 5, and Harrison started that night for Loon Lake. His arrival the next day brightened Caroline's spirits. Encouraged by "indications of improvement," he wrote Reid that if "I can see her on the way to recovery I will then be glad to put myself somewhat in the hands of friends as to any work that is demanded of me."

One essential chore was fence-mending with Platt. The New York boss was estranged not merely over what he imagined to be patronage slights but also because he felt that Harrison had never treated him as a "gentleman." As New York senator Frank Hiscock reported to the president, Platt claimed that Harrison thought it was "not the proper thing to have anything to do with me personally." Hiscock offered no explanation for this bit of paranoia, but it may well have reflected Platt's notion that the moralistic Harrison believed that Platt's involvement in a minor sex scandal a decade earlier had put him permanently beyond the pale. In any event,

Harrison opened a dialogue, writing to Platt, "I have never inten-
tionally done or omitted anything out of any personal disrespect."
He refused, however, to make any promises regarding appointments. Still, for men such as Platt who had opposed his renomination, he pledged "no penalties or disabilities—and no personal
ill-will. . . . Post convention loyalty to the ticket and to the party
should be rather the test when honors are to be distributed." In a
noncommittal response, Platt accepted Harrison's suggestion for a
meeting, and at the end of August, the two met with a few other
leaders at Reid's Westchester County farm. A few days later, Platt
told a reporter that the mutual dislike he and Harrison had harbored had been due to "misapprehension," that he would support
the ticket, and that his friends could be counted on for "hard and
steady work." A month later, in a rare speech, Platt saluted Harrison
as the party's representative and urged New York Republicans to
"Organize! organize! organize!"[44]

Harrison had hoped to make a series of speeches on his round-trip
between Loon Lake and Reid's farm, but after the conference with
Platt, he was forced to abandon the tour. Instead, he sped to Washington to coordinate the government's response to a threatened
outbreak of cholera in New York. Cases of the disease had been discovered on arriving ships carrying immigrants. Overriding state
authority, the president issued an order extending the mandatory
quarantine of ships to twenty days, and the Treasury Department
reached agreements with steamship companies to temporarily suspend immigration from infected European ports. The actions averted
an epidemic in the United States.[45]

    The political impact of the cholera scare is difficult to gauge. The
episode added fuel to the anti-immigrant propaganda campaign
of the American Protective Association and similar groups, whose
members generally favored Republicans over Democrats. Harrison
had not given the issue of immigration restriction particular prominence in his own political agenda, but neither had he done much
to resist members of his party who had. Yielding to West Coast

Republicans during the 1888 campaign, he reversed his stand on Chinese immigration and in May 1892 signed legislation extending the exclusion of Chinese laborers an additional ten years. He also signed the Immigration Act of 1891, which strengthened restrictions against entry by mentally defective persons, paupers, felons, polygamists, and "persons suffering from a loathsome or a dangerous contagious disease." During the cholera episode, however, Harrison resisted calls for a special session of Congress to pass legislation that would tighten federal quarantine regulations. Existing laws allowed for a sufficient response to this crisis, he believed, while noting that "alarm that becomes terror or panic is unwholesome and unmanly." Republican national chairman Thomas Carter assured the president that his prompt action was winning "universal applause," but it may have cost some goodwill among immigrant voters.[46]

The cholera scare—as well as the intense popular interest in the prizefight between John L. Sullivan and Jim Corbett in early September—overshadowed the release of Harrison's formal letter accepting his nomination. It was a significant blow. Caroline's illness was keeping Harrison off the stump, and the letter stood as the only substantial statement he could deliver to the voters during the campaign. He wrote the six-thousand-word document mostly at Loon Lake in the moments when he was not performing nursing duties. As Harrison surveyed the political horizon, he saw the greatest threat of defection from laborers and farmers, and he took special care in his letter to appeal to these groups.[47]

A series of violent strikes and general labor unrest also formed an inauspicious backdrop for Harrison's campaign. During the summer, union and nonunion workers squared off in the silver mines of Idaho; coal miners resisted the use of convict labor in Tennessee; steelworkers struck against the Carnegie Steel Works in Homestead, Pennsylvania; and railway switchmen walked off their jobs in Buffalo, New York. When the governor of Idaho asked Harrison for troops to ward off violence, he refused because "such a course would rather aggravate than help the situation." Only after actual fighting had broken out, several men had died, and Idaho officials had pleaded that they lacked the means to restore order did the president send troops. He used the military in none of the other strikes.[48]

The bloodiest episode occurred in Homestead, where a pitched battle between strikers and Pinkerton agents hired by the company left twelve dead and sixty wounded. Harrison thought Carnegie's manager, Henry C. Frick, had been wrong to employ the Pinker-tons. Privately, Halford noted, "The President was very emphatic against the arming of any other force than a military one with Win-chesters, and said it could not help but make bad blood." With Har-rison's approval, John Milholland, who worked for Whitelaw Reid, tried to persuade Frick to settle with the workers. Frick adamantly refused, however, and declared "with emphasis that he would never consent to settle the difficulties if President Harrison himself should personally request him to do so." The workers eventually gave up in the face of intervention by the state militia.[49]

Although Harrison did not intervene to suppress the Homestead strike, it proved damaging to his reelection campaign, not only because Andrew Carnegie had close ties with Republican leaders but even more because the strike, which was called to protest wage cuts, belied the Republicans' arguments that the protective tariff on items like steel primarily benefited labor. Nor was Harrison's cause with labor helped with Reid's presence on the ticket. In a recent dispute with printers at his newspaper, Reid had been almost as unyielding as Frick until the eve of his nomination for vice presi-dent, when a makeshift agreement was pieced together. During the campaign, a group calling itself the Labor Educational Bureau of New York distributed a pamphlet against Reid entitled *The Arch Enemy of Labor*, and Democrats generally cast their opponents as the antilabor party.[50]

Harrison faced trouble from farmers as well as labor. By 1892 the Farmers' Alliance had evolved into the Populist Party, which nominated James B. Weaver for president. The principal remedy the Populists offered to debt-ridden farmers was the free and unlimited coinage of silver at a ratio of sixteen to one with gold, and in this they enjoyed support from the silver interests of the West. During the first session of the Fifty-second Congress, when silverites revived the effort for free coinage legislation, Harrison once again made his opposition clear, prompting Colorado Republican senator Henry Teller to declare that the president "stood as the safeguard to Wall street and the money bags of that region." Harrison did initiate the calling of an international conference to discuss silver coinage at an agreed-upon ratio, but that effort did not satisfy the Populists or the silver interests, who thought that the United States could and should act alone. The Populists ran electoral tickets in nearly all the states, and in several in the West they achieved "fusion" agreements with the Democrats. "The scheme of the Fusionists," a Kansas Republican reported to the White House, "is to carry the Alliance electoral ticket at all hazards."[51]

To stanch the losses among workers and farmers, Harrison devoted most of his acceptance letter to economic issues, arguing that the "general condition of our country is one of great prosperity." On the money question, he employed phrases designed to appeal to the soft money forces of the West and the hard money forces of the East. He favored the "free coinage of silver" but only on the "one essential condition" that the two dollars must "retain an equal acceptability and value," that is, that silver coinage be limited in such fashion that the white metal remained a satellite of gold. He expressed his hope that the international silver conference, scheduled to convene after the election, would bring "highly beneficial results."

The heart of Harrison's letter was his discussion of the tariff, particularly a defense of the McKinley Tariff Act. Drawing upon the report of a bipartisan Senate investigation as well as the report of the Democratic commissioner of labor in New York State, Harrison invoked a raft of statistics to demonstrate that laborers' wages had gone up, farmers' commodity prices had risen, and the cost of articles generally used by the wage-earning classes had declined. "In view of this showing," he insisted, "it is plain that this tariff law has not imposed burdens, but has conferred benefits upon the farmer and the workingman." He noted that the Democrats in their convention had endorsed a tariff for revenue only and condemned a protective tariff as unconstitutional. He warned that the Democrats' "mad crusade against American shops" would "at once reduce the amount of work to be done in this country . . . and necessitate a reduction of . . . wages to the European standard." He also condemned the Democrats' opposition to reciprocity, a policy that had made the United States "a new and vigorous contestant" in foreign markets. Citing, for example, a vast increase in the export of American flour to Cuba, he hailed the "liberal participation of our farmers in the benefits of this policy." Appealing to agricultural regions where the Populists were making inroads, he asked, "Are the farmers of the great grain-growing States willing to surrender these new, large and increasing markets for their surplus?"[52]

Harrison intended to augment his letter with a few speeches, but even those limited plans ended in mid-September when doctors at last diagnosed Caroline Harrison as having tuberculosis. She requested that she be taken back to the White House, where on September 21 she was carried in on a stretcher, accompanied by her husband, whose "eyes, red from weeping, and with dark circles under them, told the tale of his deep distress." Mary McKee, Mame Dimmick, Russell's wife, May, and the president himself took turns watching at Mrs. Harrison's bedside as her life ebbed away.[53]

The campaign continued, although even before this sad turn of events, both Democrats and Republicans had noted how little enthusiasm the contest had generated. Some key Republicans remained aloof. Former Speaker Thomas Reed, staunchly support-ive of the president's legislative agenda but bitterly disappointed over patronage, said that he would not ride in the Harrison "ice wagon." On the day Harrison's acceptance letter appeared in news-papers, Blaine, in a scene-stealing move, issued a letter of his own defining the issues and completely ignoring the president. In a brief speech at Reid's farm and in an article in the *North American Review*, Blaine hardly mentioned his former chief. In October, former attorney general Wayne MacVeagh and Judge Walter Q. Gresham announced their intention to vote for Cleveland. Campaign leaders such as Michener sorely regretted Harrison's absence from the stump, where, Michener said, "one blast from his bugle would put every man into line." Even Harrison's daughter, Mary, wrote, "I so deeply regret Father's inability to help at this time, for if he was able to receive some delegations & make some speeches it would be a powerful factor in this canvass just as it was four years ago." But, she added, "Father would not think of leaving Mother now for anything."[54]

Caroline Harrison died on October 25, and the White House turned from vigil to mourning. With only two weeks left before the election, Harrison remained, as he later put it, "a leader in prison." Having taken his wife's body to Indianapolis for burial, he could not bring himself to go back to vote. He awaited the result with equanimity. According to Halford, "He said that he shrank from another term with its nagging annoyances, but would feel chagrined if the people of the country turned away from his administration."[55]

On Election Day, more than five million voters stood by the president, but they amounted to only 43 percent of the total. Cleveland won 46 percent, while Weaver garnered more than a million votes or 8.5 percent. Cleveland received 277 electoral votes to 145 for Harrison and 22 for Weaver. The two major doubtful states, New York and Indiana, which Harrison had carried in 1888, switched to Cleveland by narrow margins (3.4 percent in New York and 1.3 percent in Indiana). The labor issue may have injured Harrison in these industrializing states, although some observers attributed Harrison's loss to the lukewarmness of party operatives. "A certain wing of the Republican party was not sincere in its support of the President," one New Yorker reported to Halford. "To his face they were pleasant, but when he was absent [they] acted like Judas."

Harrison also narrowly lost the normally Republican states of Illinois and Wisconsin, where the labor question no doubt alienated voters in growing working-class immigrant communities. Many in those communities also held Republicans responsible for recent state legislation hostile to immigrant parochial schools, and Harrison's actions during the cholera scare may have aggravated those feelings. Catholics also deeply resented Harrison's commissioner of Indian affairs for moving to establish secular schools on reservations where Catholic institutions had been predominant under the contract system.

In the West, the money issue hurt Harrison. In Colorado, Idaho, and Kansas, the Democrats had entered into fusion with the Populists, whose electors for Weaver proved victorious. In Nevada, anti-Harrison silver Republicans allied with the Populists and defeated both the Democrats and regular Republicans. In California, which had gone Democratic only once since 1856, Cleveland won 8 of 9 electors. Nationwide, Cleveland's plurality was 363,000 votes, and the Democrats also won a majority in both houses of Congress.[56]

After the election, Harrison's mailbag brought a host of post-mortem explanations for his loss: the Homestead strike, Reid's labor record, the silver revolt, the McKinley Tariff and the high-price bogey, Catholic and immigrant opposition, lingering paranoia over the Lodge Federal Elections Bill, Democratic fraud in some districts, patronage grudges, factional animosities, and lethargy among Republican cadres. Given the nation's diverse voting population, the winner-take-all electoral system, and an evenly divided electorate, all of these factors no doubt contributed in some degree to the outcome.[57]

Harrison thought there "were many influences, some great and some small, which combined to produce the result." Most significantly, he wrote to Reid, "The workingman declined to walk under the protective umbrella because it sheltered his employer also. He has smashed it for the fun of seeing the silk stockings take rain." The campaign may have suffered from "faults of management," but Harrison engaged in no recrimination against fellow Republicans, though regretting his own forced inactivity. "I was so removed from the campaign that I can scarcely realize that I was a candidate," he wrote one supporter. Still, he admitted "no sting" at his defeat. "It does not seem to me," he confessed, "that I could have had the physical strength to go through what would have been before me if I had been re-elected, with the added burden of a great personal grief. I have often said that I did not want to die in a public building or to have an official funeral." "I have never enjoyed public life," he wrote to another friend, and "do not seem to have the mental adaptation which would enable me to get satisfaction out of it. I always carry care and responsibility heavily."[58]

Harrison turned from election analyses to his last great responsibility, preparation of his fourth annual message. Expecting no action from Congress, he determined to use the document as a brief for Republican policies. Although he might feel little sorrow over his own loss, he wrote to friends that he would "greatly regret to see the tariff, reciprocity and shipping legislation destroyed" and the abandonment of "other progressive movements." Despite the apparent judgment of the people, Harrison remained convinced that his administration had served their interests well.

As he had in his letter of acceptance, Harrison offered a profusion of statistics to demonstrate the nation's unprecedented and widespread prosperity. The election outcome suggested that many Americans saw things differently, but he said, "If any are discontented with their state here, if any believe that wages or prices, the returns for honest toil, are inadequate, they should not fail to remember that there is no other country in the world where the conditions that seem to them hard would not be accepted as highly prosperous." He advocated continued support for sound money, an expanded merchant marine, and increased trade, but he focused most on the protective tariff, which he described as "a most powerful agency in protecting the homes of our workingmen from the invasion of want." Unfortunately, in the recent campaign, "disturbed relations" between workers and employers had "not been favorable to a calm consideration by the wage earner of the effect upon wages of the protective system. The facts that his wages were the highest paid in like callings in the world and that a maintenance of this rate of wages in the absence of protective duties upon the product of his labor was impossible were obscured by the passion evoked by these contests." Harrison conceded that the Democrats would institute a new policy, and the worker would then be able to assess his "personal experience under the operation of a tariff for revenue only." This was but one of many Democratic policies that threatened the nation's well-being, however. As he contemplated the consequences of his adversaries' overturning what the Republicans had accomplished, the president solemnly intoned in his last sentence, "Retrogression would be a crime."[59]

Harrison expected this discussion of domestic policy to stand as a sort of political testament, but, at the very close of his administration, foreign affairs again took center stage. In mid-January discontent in Hawaii finally boiled over in a revolution that ousted Queen Liliuokalani. Led by nonnative, mostly American-descended lawyers, planters, and businessmen, the antiroyalists justified their action by the queen's intention to promulgate a new constitution to enlarge the political power of native Hawaiians at the expense of foreigners. Although the queen quickly backed down, the revolutionaries proceeded with their work, aided by the landing of U.S. troops from a nearby warship and the hasty recognition of their provisional government by American minister John L. Stevens, a longtime advocate of an American takeover of the islands. A delegation of commissioners soon set off for Washington, where by February 14, 1893, they and Secretary of State Foster had completed a treaty of annexation.

No evidence suggests that Harrison engineered or even expected this development, but he was fully prepared to take advantage of the offer. The queen complained that Stevens had aided the revolutionaries, and she asked Harrison not to act until he had heard the full story. He ignored her pleas. Sending the treaty to the Senate, he claimed that the "overthrow of the monarchy was not in any way promoted by this Government." He said the "restoration of Queen Liliuokalani to her throne is undesirable, if not impossible," and would be "accompanied by serious disaster and the disorganization of all business interests." Arguing that the "influence and interest of the United States in the islands must be increased and not diminished," he saw annexation as the only course that would "adequately secure the interests of the United States." Nonetheless, revelations regarding Stevens's conduct and the arrival in America of the queen's representative to tell her story raised doubts. Democratic and independent newspapers questioned the haste of the treaty negotiations. In the crowded days at the end of the congressional session, the Senate chose to take no action before Harrison left office.[60]

On March 4, Harrison and Cleveland rode by carriage from the White House to Capitol Hill as they had on that rainy day four years earlier. Their roles were now reversed. President Cleveland took the oath of office. Four hours later, private citizen Benjamin Harrison took a train for Indianapolis.

---

# 7

# "The Curtain Is Down"

In March 1893 Benjamin Harrison stepped down from the presidency at age fifty-nine, exhausted by four years of hard work but not quite ready to retire. Once again he planned to hang out his lawyer's shingle. He had "not lost any interest in the Republican party" and would continue to defend its principles, but, he insisted, "There is nothing further from my mind or thought or wish than the resumption of public office." Although a huge crowd greeted him at Indianapolis, he found that "sad memories almost obscured the light of the welcoming smiles of my old neighbors." His first day home, he put flowers on Caroline's grave. Yet, even though he came home a widower, Harrison could still relish his deliverance from "the hard and sad experiences of the last year." At last, he wrote to Elijah Halford, "the shake is going out of my pen."[1]

Mary Harrison McKee and her two children accompanied Harrison and remained with him several months. Father and daughter soon threw themselves into a complete refurbishing of the Delaware Street house. Mary selected paints and wallpapers and supervised workmen, while Harrison unpacked his books and papers and turned his library into an office. Young Benjamin and his sister, Mary Lodge, put in some work in the garden, although Ben much preferred a game of ball with his doting grandfather.

Despite all the frenzied activity and the diversion of the children, Harrison nonetheless felt a sense of emptiness in his personal life. The first letter he wrote from Delaware Street was to Mame Dimmick, who still occupied a special place in his affections and whose assistance in caring for Caroline had earned his "gratitude and love." Worried that her "excitement & labors" had damaged her health, Harrison urged Mame to "do what I am going to do—get the nerves under control." Within weeks, he invited her to Indianapolis where she could get "quite fixed up after the very trying year we have had."[2]

The invitation was a shock to Mary McKee. "I have refrained from writing Mame D.," Mary wrote to her husband, Robert, "& surely thought my silence would be taken as hint enough that she was not wanted by *me* at least. Father I suppose gave her such an *urgent* invitation, however, that here she is." "I am keeping calm & abiding [sic] my time," Mary added, "but the day will come yet when Father will realize his treatment of his children has been anything *but kind*."

Given Harrison's remarkable generosity toward his children, this last statement is astonishing and can have been rooted only in the McKees' extreme resentment of Mame Dimmick. Such a strong feeling, expressed so soon after leaving the White House, indicates that Mary McKee had come to dislike her cousin intensely during the years in Washington. Many years later, Robert McKee alleged that Caroline Harrison had grown disturbed by the relationship between her husband and her niece and had threatened to leave the president. But the contemporary correspondence and Mame's diary provide no evidence that Mrs. Harrison and Mrs. Dimmick did not get along. As late as June 25, 1891, the first lady, who was at the seashore, wrote a very cordial letter to her niece, who was in Washington with the president. Mame often helped her aunt with social duties and correspondence, and no evidence indicates that Mrs. Harrison objected to the young woman's faithful ministrations during her last illness.

More plausibly, it was Mary McKee rather than her mother who thought that Mame was taking her own place in Harrison's affections. Certainly, the president enjoyed Mame's company. Mary did not like exercise; Mame did, and she and the president often took walks and played billiards. Mary was fussy about social matters—something that did not interest her father. A month after Caroline died and three months before leaving Washington, Mary had written to Robert that "at times it seems as if I could not endure that state of things a moment longer, but I am trying to follow the Bible rule of *great* patience. As I told you, dear, it can not possibly last much longer & I do not want to loose [*sic*] my patience these last *few weeks* when I have kept my temper *so long*." Mary conceded that it might have been a mistake to spend those years with her parents rather than her husband, "but I loved my Father & Mother dearly & thought I could please & make *all* happy. I can not yet believe that all my work & efforts will go for naught & so as I said before must keep my patience awhile longer."

Now, with Mame Dimmick visiting at Delaware Street in the spring of 1893, Mary McKee's patience was further tried. She made the best of it, however, and maintained peace, while Harrison failed to detect or chose to ignore the tensions. "We have all enjoyed her presence," Harrison wrote to Mame's sister Lizzie. Mame and Lizzie spent that summer at Harrison's cottage in Cape May, after which Harrison wrote to Mame from Indianapolis, "I will be glad always to have you visit me here. . . . Let me hear from you often and do not want for anything I can do for you."[3]

As the onerous duties of the presidency receded, Harrison moved to resume the practice of law. He accepted only a small number of clients and earned fees sometimes ranging as high as twenty-five thousand dollars. He also began to write for publication, again receiving handsome fees for articles placed in middle-class magazines. As for politics, he privately groused about Grover Cleveland's policies and blunders. Particularly galling was Cleveland's appointment of Walter Q. Gresham as secretary of state. Five days after taking office, Cleveland and Gresham withdrew Harrison's Hawaiian annexation treaty from the Senate. After a State Department investigation found Americans culpable in the queen's ouster, Cleveland made a halfhearted and unsuccessful attempt to restore her to power, a move Harrison branded as "most humiliating to our country." "[T]he dusky Queen . . . ought to make a royal visit to Washington," Harrison sneered privately. "The Pres[iden]t could call on her without any loss of dignity."[4]

Harrison also watched scornfully as Cleveland struggled ineptly with the Panic of 1893 and the ensuing depression. Like many Republicans, Harrison believed that the economic crisis derived in large part from business fears of impending tariff reductions by the Democrats. Hence, he correctly predicted that Cleveland's proposed immediate solution, repeal of the Sherman Silver Purchase Act, would "not work the wonders that many have believed." In fact, the depression deepened and set the stage for a dramatic Republican comeback, which began in the 1893 state elections in New York, Pennsylvania, Ohio, and elsewhere. Again condemning the Democrats' threats to protectionism, Harrison told reporters that the election "result demonstrates that the faith of the people in the American industrial system was not lost, but only weakened, and has been renewed with redoubled strength." A year after leaving office, Harrison took obvious pride when he learned that "a man who is engaged in work among the poor in New York City" reported that "he finds my picture in many of their houses & that they speak of me with great kindness & of the good times they had during my administration."[5]

Harrison had taken little part in the 1893 campaign, devoting his time instead to preparing a series of law lectures for delivery at Stanford University the next year. In the long intervals when no family members were with him, he had few diversions. "It is fearfully lonesome in this empty house," he wrote to Mame Dimmick. "I have not gotten into visiting habits & it is very rare that any one comes in, so my evenings are spent alone—with a book or in none too cheerful reverie." "What a quick good walk we could have if you were here," he wrote in early December. "Cheeks and (Shall I say it) more aglow and hearts alive to the good things of God."[6]

In the spring, Mary McKee and her children accompanied Harrison on his trip to Stanford, where he delivered six lectures on the early development of the American Constitution. The students gave the novice professor "very generous applause," he wrote to Mame after his first lecture, "but still I felt a sort of sense of failure. . . . I needed you to cheer me up." The pious Presbyterian Harrison was dismayed to find "no excess of religious influence about the university." In the White House, he had striven to maintain his religious values even while the crush of duties encroached on formal observances. Now that he had more time, his spiritual concerns reasserted themselves. Thus, when he attended a college church service where a lay speaker denied the universality of the soul and said that heaven was "the myth of the Savages," Harrison was "outraged" and "so indignant that I could hardly sit still." A few weeks later, he agreed to speak to the campus YMCA to try to "do some good." California offered opportunities for interesting side trips, but after two months, Harrison was ready to head east. Once home, he set off immediately to see Mame in New York. The visit deepened their mutual regard. Back in Indianapolis in June 1894, in a second letter within a day, Harrison wrote, "Why do I write at all, just because I love you & it is just a little like being with you, & this gives me pleasure."[7]

Harrison was finding renewed spirit, but the nation's economic depression showed no signs of easing. He deplored the mounting discontent among workers and farmers. "What a strange and threatening thing this 'Commonweal Army' has become. . . . I am glad," he wrote with a touch of amnesia, "that such incidents of want and social disturbance did not characterize my administration." He blamed the troubles on the Democrats' failed policies, and he made that case publicly in his work during the 1894 congressional election campaigns. Rejecting the idea "that the only appropriate habiliment of an ex-president was mummy-cloth," he made scores of speeches in Indiana and a major address at Carnegie Hall in New York. Focusing again on the tariff, he spoke of "the enormous losses that have fallen upon the country" as a result of the Democrats' bungled attempt at revision with the Wilson-Gorman Act, which not only jeopardized protection but also abrogated Harrison's reciprocity agreements. Most lamentable was the grim prospect that wages would fall "so low that hope would go out of the heart of the man who toils in the mill. Unless there is hope in the heart [and] some promise of better things," he warned, "you may expect anarchy and social disorders."[8]

In a reversal of the trend in 1890 and 1892, the Republicans won a landslide victory in 1894, which Harrison called "the most extraordinary political revolution the country has ever witnessed." "The workingmen voted their prejudices in 1892," he told reporters; "this year they voted their patriotism and their love of home." Harrison's services in the campaign inevitably inspired calls for his renomination for the presidency two years hence; he politely turned them aside. "It is pleasant to be called before the curtain," he wrote to Mame, "but . . . a bow will do—the curtain is down."[9]

In late 1894 and early 1895, Harrison chose instead to throw himself into a complicated will case in Richmond, sixty-five miles east of Indianapolis. He found the work away from home exacting and exhausting. He wrote to Mame, "If you were here I would ask you to rub my head—not to talk—for my ears and brain are again in the old condition of the campaign of 1888, and of many of my days at the White House. . . . You were quick to understand these moods and to comply with them." In March 1895 the rigors of the case took their toll, and Harrison fell ill with the grippe, what later generations called influenza. Mary McKee rushed from New York to Indianapolis, and much to her dismay, Mame Dimmick went with her. "Father has never shown me greater affection," Mary wrote to her husband, but as for Mame, "I freely confess that I so *thoroughly* despise the woman that I *can not* form an unbiased opinion nor a *wise* one." For his part, Harrison was "delighted that Mame D. came along," and so once again Mary raised no row that would add to her father's troubles. In her agitated state, she wrote to Robert, "Two conclusions only can be reached as I have said before, either they are in love & intend to marry or they intend that I have got to *accept* her or make a break. It is a mystery to me to know which." By that time, Harrison was in fact deeply in love with Mame, although he had not yet sorted out the question of marriage. After a few weeks under the two women's care, Harrison recovered. He returned to court, won the will case, and collected a fee of twenty-five thousand dollars.[10]

As the 1896 campaign approached, speculation about a Harrison presidential nomination persisted. The notion received no encouragement from the putative candidate, who continued to concentrate on his lucrative law practice. "Power has some compensations," he had concluded, "but no joys in itself." For the *Ladies Home Journal*, he wrote a series of articles on the workings of the national government with the professed aim of promoting "an intelligent patriotism." (The articles later appeared as a book entitled, *This Country of Ours*.) In his discussion of the presidency, he described the White House as "an office and a home combined—an evil combination" that offered "no break in the day—no change of atmosphere" between public and private life.[11]

And private life was at the forefront of Harrison's agenda. He spent the summer of 1895 in the Adirondack Mountains, where he invited his family to join him at a cabin that he hopefully dubbed "Camp Reconciliation." He spoke "very strongly" to Mary and Robert to be on their good behavior regarding Mame. Whatever peace he achieved, however, ended in November when he finally told his children of his intention to marry in April 1896. Both Mrs. McKee and her brother, Russell, vehemently opposed the match, but Harrison assured Mame, "They and you shall find me true to you." He publicly announced the engagement in January, and newspapers pounced on the rumored family split. In an especially scurrilous piece, the Democratic *New York World* claimed that during his administration a "quarrel" between Harrison and Caroline over Mrs. Dimmick had grown "critical" but had not become public because of Mrs. Harrison's "own good sense and the efforts of her son and daughter, who were horrified at the prospect of a 'White House scandal.'" Given the inclusion of some fairly obscure details, the story apparently was planted by a family member, most likely Robert McKee. Whatever the source, Harrison assured Mame, "we can sustain each other through such annoyances & greater ones."[12]

With the Republican National Convention just a few months away, observers wondered what impact the impending marriage might have on Harrison's chances for a third nomination. In late January the Indiana Republican state committee endorsed the former president for reelection, but he moved swiftly to decline all consideration. In a public letter to the committee chairman, he declared, "There never has been an hour since I left the White House that I have felt a wish to return to it."[13]

While the friends of actual candidates jockeyed for whatever legacy of support he might leave, Harrison proceeded with his marital plans. "How selfish it is," he wrote to Mame, "that anyone should want to deny me your presence and love when I so sorely need them." March was an anguished time at Delaware Street, as Mary and Russell showed up to remove their possessions from the family home. Robert McKee was in town as well, although he did not step foot in the house or allow his wife to stay there. "His malice and his mendacity run neck & neck," said Harrison. In some ways, most wrenching to Harrison was grandson Ben's "promise that he would always love me. It broke me up very much." Harrison loved his children deeply, but he wrote to Mame, "We have done all we could, save to give each other up, to please them and that no one had a right to ask." On April 6, 1896, Harrison and Mame Dimmick were married in a small private ceremony at her Episcopal church in New York. On February 21, 1897, Mame gave birth to Harrison's third child, Elizabeth.[14]

While Harrison and his bride were settling in at Delaware Street, the Republicans were preparing for their national convention in St. Louis, where William McKinley won an easy first-ballot nomination.

Harrison did not share the delegates' enthusiasm for the nominee, who he thought lacked "a firm will." McKinley borrowed Harrison's technique of the front-porch campaign, but the ex-president did not rush onto the stump, telling one friend, "If I am to be a political hack, I had as well have been a candidate." Once again, he consented to give a speech at Carnegie Hall. He made only one brief mention of McKinley, however, and spent most of his time denouncing Democratic nominee William Jennings Bryan and his free-silver panacea, which Harrison described as "the financial and moral equivalent of a declaration that fifty-cent pieces are dollars." (After Harrison's death, Mrs. Harrison published this speech and other writings in a book, *Views of an Ex-President*.) Harrison also spoke in Richmond, Charleston, West Virginia, and Cincinnati, as well as making a brief speaking tour through Indiana. But McKinley hardly needed Harrison's help; he defeated Bryan handily.[15]

In 1897 Harrison undertook the most noted and arduous assignment of his entire legal career—service as chief counsel for Venezuela in its dispute with Great Britain over the boundary separating Venezuela from the British colony of Guiana. The origin of the long-standing dispute extended back to the ambiguity of boundary and title of the original Spanish and Dutch territories that were now held by Venezuela and Britain. For decades, Venezuela had sought American aid in getting Britain to agree to arbitration, and under pressure from the Cleveland administration, the British finally acceded. Harrison's task was to prepare the Venezuelan case for the Tribunal of Arbitration set to meet in Paris in 1899. He earned his eighty-thousand-dollar fee. Although assisted by associate counsel, Harrison bore the brunt of the labor for the better part of two years, often to the exclusion of virtually all other legal work. Through 1897 and 1898, he and his team produced a multivolume printed argument preparatory to oral arguments the next year.[16]

While assembling a case that challenged British imperial pretensions, Harrison grew increasingly uncomfortable with such pretensions on the part of his own country. He accepted the Spanish-American War launched by McKinley as a "war for human-

ity" to rescue Cuba from oppressive Spanish rule, but he denied
that the United States had "God's commission to deliver the
oppressed the world around." Less than three weeks after Com-
modore George Dewey's victory in Manila, Harrison expressed
concern over American ambitions in the Philippines. He excused
his own administration's attempted annexation of Hawaii on the
grounds that it was something offered to, not sought by, the United
States. Taking the Philippines, however, would violate the long-
standing policy, embodied in the Monroe Doctrine, that the United
States should "leave the rest of the world alone." "Why should we
do anything more than to secure a snug little harbor for a coaling
station?" he asked. "We must have coaling stations in various parts
of the world, but I do not think we want, with these, extensive territories." In the 1898 midterm elections, Harrison did not campaign
for Republican candidates. He pleaded that the Venezuela case left
him no time, but, he wrote to a friend, "I am not right sure that I
find myself in sympathy with the extreme expansion views that are
being advocated." In the end, the United States acquired from
Spain not only the Philippines but Puerto Rico and Guam as well.[17]

In 1899 Harrison took his new family to Paris for the oral arguments in the boundary arbitration. The tribunal's judges included
two Britons, two Americans, and a Russian. After months of tedious
proceedings, Harrison presented the last argument in September,
talking for twenty-five hours over five days. Within a week, the tribunal returned a unanimous decision awarding the lion's share
of the disputed territory to Great Britain. Harrison was certain that
the British judges had pressured the Russian to give in to British
demands and had threatened to give Venezuela no territory at all
unless the Americans agreed to make the award unanimous. Embit-
tered at the result, he wrote, "Law is nothing to a British judge it
seems when it is a matter of extending British dominion."[18]

Similarly, Harrison was troubled by America's exercise of
dominion over its own new territories. He continued to believe that
acquisition of the Philippines was "a sad mistake." In March 1900
when the Republican Congress considered levying a tariff on goods

from Puerto Rico, he concluded that "a brief word of dissent from me was in the line of duty." Treating the territory unequally, he declared, would be "a most serious departure from right principles." Administration Republicans criticized him roundly, but privately he was even more damning. "It seems to me," he wrote to John W. Foster, "that the proposition that the Congress of the United States has absolute power over the lives and property of large bodies of civilized people is a shocking one and I cannot believe that the framers of our constitution, who were so careful to restrain the powers of Congress, could have contemplated such a use of them." He refused to speak for McKinley in his second contest with Bryan in 1900, largely because it "seems as if some of our Republican orators were arguing a bill of exceptions to the Declaration of Independence." After McKinley appointed him to a largely honorific seat on the new International Court at the Hague, Harrison only half-jokingly excused his campaign silence by the rule that a judge should "not drag the ermine in the pool of politics!" Near the end of the campaign, he issued a canned interview in which he stood by his position on the territories, hailed the return of prosperity under Republican economic policies, and argued not so much for McKinley's election as against Bryan's.[19]

Harrison's opposition to McKinley's imperialism reflected a general anxiety he felt over the nation's direction in these late years. The depression of the mid-nineties had posed a severe test of American institutions, but the ill-distributed prosperity that followed was equally threatening to American virtue. Harrison worried that a "canker of greed" had "eaten into the hearts" of the rising generation of Americans. Giving increased attention to church work in the last years of his life, he believed that "to the word of God and the church of the Lord Jesus Christ must we turn for the hope that men may be delivered from this consuming greed and selfishness." He condemned the fierce competition among corporations that led them to squeeze profits out of labor, and he denounced inequities such as the widespread evasion of property taxes by the wealthy.

Like Social Gospel exponents, Harrison hoped for a moral regeneration in politics. In that sense, he had come full circle to his first affinity for the Republican party. Two months before his death, he wrote to a friend, "In the old Republican days the subject of slavery and of the saving of the Union made appeals to the consciences and liberty-loving instincts of the people." Now, citing one of McKinley's campaign emblems, he said, "These later years have been full of talk about commerce and dinner pails, but I feel sure that the American conscience and the American love of liberty have not been smothered. They will break through this crust of sordidness and realize that those only keep their liberties who accord liberty to others."[20]

In early March 1901, Harrison again fell ill with an acute case of the grippe, which soon progressed into pneumonia. With his wife of five years the only family member at his bedside, he died on March 13, 1901. The next day, President McKinley issued a proclamation of mourning, noting that in "the high office of President," Harrison had "displayed extraordinary gifts as administrator and statesman."[21]

To himself, McKinley perhaps also acknowledged that he owed something of his own success in the White House to the example Harrison had set. Benjamin Harrison had not set out to transform the presidency, but he was hardly a mere caretaker between the two terms of Grover Cleveland. In his own right, Harrison made important contributions to the evolution of the office. He entered the presidency strongly committed to a set of principles and policies. In defense of those ideas and in pursuit of what he thought to be his duty, he expanded the boundaries of presidential activism. Both publicly and behind the scenes, he effectively intervened in the deliberations of Congress and posted a remarkable record of legislative achievement. He resisted the dictation of party bosses in the matter of appointments, thereby risking his own reelection for the sake of presidential independence. He frequently operated as the nation's chief diplomat and shaped its aspirations in foreign affairs. Through a skillful use of the press and in widespread travels he took the presidency to the American people. In these and other ways, he unwittingly taught his successors new uses of power and techniques of leadership. The solipsistic and ham-handed Grover Cleveland took few cues from Harrison, but William McKinley proved one of his most astute students. As a member of the Fifty-first Congress, McKinley watched Harrison firsthand. A half decade later, borrowing much from Harrison's methods and purposes but unburdened by many of his obstacles and shortcomings, McKinley fashioned a popular and successful administration. Scholars may regard the latter man as the first modern president, but Benjamin Harrison had clearly pointed the way.

# Notes

ABBREVIATIONS IN NOTES

ANB—*American National Biography.* Edited by John A. Garraty and Mark C. Carnes. 24 vols. New York, 1999.

BFT—Benjamin Franklin Tracy. BFT-LC—Benjamin Franklin Tracy Papers, Library of Congress, Washington, DC.

BH—Benjamin Harrison.

BH-Home—Benjamin Harrison Papers, Benjamin Harrison Home, Indianapolis.

BH-IHS—Benjamin Harrison Papers, Indiana Historical Society, Indianapolis.

BH-LC—Benjamin Harrison Papers, Library of Congress.

BH-Walker—Benjamin Harrison Papers, Collection of Benjamin Harrison Walker, privately held.

CR—*Congressional Record,* cited with Congress, session, and pages.

CSH—Caroline Scott Harrison.

EWH—Elijah W. Halford.

FRUS—*Foreign Relations of the United States,* cited with year and pages.

GFH—George F. Hoar. GFH-MHS—George F. Hoar Papers, Massachusetts Historical Society, Boston.

HCL—Henry Cabot Lodge. HCL-MHS—Henry Cabot Lodge Papers, Massachusetts Historical Society.

IJ—*Indianapolis Journal.*

IMH—*Indiana Magazine of History.*

JAA—John A. Anderson.

JCS—John C. Spooner. JCS-LC—John C. Spooner Papers, Library of Congress.

JGB—James G. Blaine. JGB-LC—James G. Blaine Papers, Library of Congress.

JRM—J. Robert McKee.

JS—John Sherman. JS-LC—John Sherman Papers, Library of Congress.

JSC—James S. Clarkson.

JSH—John Scott Harrison.

JWF—John W. Foster.

LC—Library of Congress.

LTM—Louis T. Michener. LTM-LC—Louis T. Michener Papers, Library of Congress.

MHM—Mary Harrison McKee.

MLH—Mary Lord Harrison: Mary (Mame) Scott Dimmick until April 6, 1896.

MSD—Mary (Mame) Scott Dimmick: Mary Lord Harrison after April 6, 1896.

MWP—Margaret W. Peltz.

NYT—*New York Times.*

NYTr—*New York Tribune.*

OR—*The War of the Rebellion: A Compilation of the Official Records of the Union and Confederate Armies,* cited with volume and page. All citations are to series I.

SBE—Stephen B. Elkins. SBE-WVU—Stephen B. Elkins Papers, West Virginia University Library, Morgantown.

TCP—Thomas C. Platt. TCP-Yale—Thomas C. Platt Papers, Yale University Library, New Haven.

WHHM—William Henry Harrison Miller.

WQG—Walter Q. Gresham. WQG-LC—Walter Q. Gresham Papers, Library of Congress.

WR—Whitelaw Reid. WR-LC—Reid Family Papers, Library of Congress.

INTRODUCTION

1. Henry Adams, *The Education of Henry Adams* (1918; reprint: Boston: Houghton Mifflin, 1961), 321.

2. Charles Hedges, comp., *Speeches of Benjamin Harrison* (New York: United States Book Company, 1892), 448.

3. Adams, *Education,* 324.

1: "A HARD-EARNED LOAF"

1. Norman K. Risjord, "Harrison, Benjamin," ANB, 10:197–98.

2. Bernard Friedman, "William Henry Harrison: The People against the Parties," in *Gentlemen from Indiana: National Party Candidates, 1836–1940,* ed. Ralph D. Gray (Indianapolis: Indiana Historical Bureau, 1977), 3–28; Michael F. Holt, *The Rise and Fall of the American Whig Party* (New York: Oxford University Press, 1999), 41–42, 45, 89–113.

3. Kenneth R. Stevens, "William Henry Harrison," in *Buckeye Presidents: Ohioans in the White House,* ed. Philip Weeks (Kent, Ohio: Kent State University Press, 2003), 35–37.

4. Harry J. Sievers, *Benjamin Harrison*, 3 vols. (vols. 1 and 2: New York: University Publishers, 1952, 1959; vol. 3: Indianapolis: Bobbs-Merrill, 1968), 1:20–22, 29–30.

5. Sievers, *Harrison*, 1:16–19.

6. Sievers, *Harrison*, 1:22–23, 26–27; Lew Wallace, *Life of Gen. Ben Harrison* (Philadelphia: Hubbard Brothers, 1888), 54–55.

7. Sievers, *Harrison*, 1:27–29; Wallace, *Life of Harrison*, 58.

8. Sievers, *Harrison*, 1:25–26.

9. Sievers, *Harrison*, 1:29–33; Boyd T. Reese, Jr., "Bishop, Robert Hamilton," ANB, 2:834–35.

10. BH, undated essays, Farmers' College, late 1840s, BH-LC.

11. BH, "Composition No. 9 Dr. Bishop," n.d., BH-LC.

12. Sievers, *Harrison*, 1:45–48; Ophia D. Smith, "Caroline Scott Harrison: A Daughter of Old Oxford," *National Historical Magazine* 75 (1941): 5–6; BH to JSH, June 9, 1850, BH-Walker.

13. Sievers, *Harrison*, 1:46–50, 55–58; Wallace, *Life of Harrison*, 61.

14. Harrison's college writings are in BH-LC.

15. Sievers, *Harrison*, 1:58–63; BH, speech manuscript, April 28, 1851, and undated, untitled essay, circa 1851–52, BH-LC.

16. "Miami University. Programme of the Exercises on Commencement Day. June 24, 1852," BH, "England's poor—June 24th 1852," manuscript, BH-LC.

17. Sievers, *Harrison*, 1:67–70; *Appletons' Cyclopaedia of American Biography* (New York: D. Appleton and Company, 1891), 5:706.

18. Sievers, *Harrison*, 1:72–82; BH to JAA, August 25, September 24, 1853, BH to John W. Scott, October 5, 1853, BH-LC.

19. Sievers, *Harrison*, 1: 84–87; BH to JAA, October 10, 1853, William Sheets to BH, March 18, 1854, BH-LC.

20. Sievers, *Harrison*, 1:88–94, 98.

21. BH to CSH, September 19, 1854, BH-Home; Sievers, *Harrison*, 1:95–107; Wallace, *Life of Harrison*, 72–77.

22. Sievers, *Harrison*, 1:110–114; BH, notes in *Diary, Memorandum Book, and Almanac for 1858*, BH-LC.

23. Sievers, *Harrison*, 1:114–125.

24. *Benjamin Harrison Memorial*, House Document No. 154, 77th Cong., 1st sess., 127–28; JAA to BH, October 2, 1856, BH to JAA, October 10, 1853, November 5, 1856, BH-LC.

25. Sievers, *Harrison*, 1:127–34; Charles Zimmerman, "The Origin and Rise of the Republican Party in Indiana from 1854 to 1860," IMH 13 (1917): 362–71.

26. Sievers, *Harrison*, 1:136–53; BH, "1860 Campaign Notes," "Speeches made during Canvass for Reporter Sup court 1860," BH-LC.

27. Sievers, *Harrison*, 1:156–68; JSH to BH, February 7, 1861, BH-LC.

28. Wallace, *Life of Harrison*, 180; Sievers, *Harrison*, 1:178–87; James M. Perry, *Touched with Fire* (New York: Public Affairs, 2003), 16; BH to CSH, August 21, 1862, BH-LC.

29. Sievers, *Harrison*, 1:188–233.

30. BH to CSH, November 21, 28, December 4, 7, 1862, February 26, 1863, BH-LC.
31. BH to CSH, November 21, December 24, 27, 1862, January 11, March 26, 1863, BH-LC; *Short Review of the Public and Private Life of Gen'l Benj. Harrison* (n.p., 1888), 14.
32. Sievers, *Harrison*, 1:228–230; BH to CSH, August 25, October 8, November 27, 1863, April 7, 1864, BH-LC.
33. Sievers, *Harrison*, 1:242–53; BH to CSH, May [14] [misdated], 20, June 14, 1864, BH-LC.
34. Sievers, *Harrison*, 1:254–56; Wallace, *Life of Harrison*, 202; *Benjamin Harrison Memorial*, 114; BH to CSH, June 18, 1864, BH-LC; Lorna Lutes Sylvester, "'Gone for a Soldier': The Civil War Letters of Charles Harding Cox," IMH 68 (1972): 212.
35. Sievers, *Harrison*, 1:258–64; BH to CSH, August 20, 1864, BH to E. A. Carman, February 8, 1876, BH-LC.
36. Sievers, *Harrison*, 1:264–77.
37. OR, vol. 45, pt. 1, 519–24.
38. Sievers, *Harrison*, 1:289–99; OR, vol. 47, pt.1, 792–94.
39. BH to CSH, November 30, December 4, 1862, March 17, May 21, 1865, BH-LC.

2: THE PATH TO FUTURE FRUIT

1. BH to CSH, June 18, 1864, BH-LC; IJ, August 12, 1865.
2. Sievers, *Harrison*, 2:9–12, 18–21.
3. IJ, June 1, 1871; Sievers, 2:35–45.
4. IJ, February 23, 1872; Sievers, 2:48–59.
5. Sievers, *Harrison*, 2:66–68; Charles W. Calhoun, "Caroline Lavinia Scott Harrison," in *American First Ladies: Their Lives and Their Legacy*, 2nd ed., ed. Lewis L. Gould (New York: Routledge, 2001), 174.
6. BH to MWP, November 26, 1886, BH-LC.
7. Irwin Unger, *The Greenback Era* (Princeton: Princeton University Press, 1964); Gretchen Ritter, *Goldbugs and Greenbacks* (Cambridge, England: Cambridge University Press, 1997).
8. Newspaper clipping, n.d., Scrapbook No. 1, BH-LC.
9. Sievers, *Harrison*, 2:86–92.
10. Sievers, *Harrison*, 2:79–87; JSH to BH, January 19, 1876, BH-LC.
11. Sievers, *Harrison*, 2:95–107.
12. IJ, August 19, 24, September 6, 27, October 2, 3, 1876; *Indianapolis News*, August 21, 1876; newspaper clipping, n.d., Scrapbook No. 3, BH-LC.
13. Sievers, *Harrison*, 2:122–28, 131–34.
14. *Indianapolis News*, July 23–August 4, 1877; Sergeant Wappenhaus to chief signal officer, July 24–26, 1877, Albert J. Meyer to the president and secretary of war, July 28–30, 1877, Rutherford B. Hayes Papers, Hayes Presidential Center, Fremont, Ohio; BH, militia oath with note,

July 27, 1877, BH to Thomas Drummond, August 16, 20, 1877, BH-LC.

15. IJ, June 6, August 10, 1878; Sievers, *Harrison*, 2:141–62; Allan Pinkerton to BH, June, 1878, BH-Walker.

16. BH to MWP, October 11, 1878, BH-LC; Sievers, *Harrison*, 2:165–67.

17. IJ, March 9, 1880.

18. *Proceedings of the Republican National Convention . . . 1880* (Chicago: Jno. B. Jeffrey Printing and Publishing House, 1881), 197–271, 279; Sievers, *Harrison*, 2:168–73.

19. Sievers, *Harrison*, 2:178–83; BH to MWP, September 1, October 13, 18, 1880, BH-LC.

20. Charles W. Calhoun, *Gilded Age Cato: The Life of Walter Q. Gresham* (Lexington, Ky.: University Press of Kentucky, 1988), 56–62.

21. BH to MWP, March 29, 1882, December 15, 1886, BH-LC.

22. IJ, August 30, 1882; CR, 47–1, 639.

23. IJ, August 31, 1882; newspaper clipping, n.d., Scrapbook No. 2, BH-LC.

24. CR, 47th Cong., 1st sess., 1013, 48th Cong., 1st sess., 1338, 5043–44; BH to F. H. Huron, December 10, 1885, BH-LC; Sievers, *Harrison*, 2:209–210; Mary R. Dearing, *Veterans in Politics* (Baton Rouge: Louisiana State University Press, 1952), 284–87.

25. CR, 47th Cong., 1st sess., 2983–88, 3134–39; Charles Latham, Jr., "Benjamin Harrison in the Senate, 1881–1887" (senior thesis, Princeton University, 1939), 69–79.

26. CR, 48th Cong., 1st sess., 2243–44, 2341, 2693–2707, 2724; BH to William Bosson, March 11, 1886, BH-LC.

27. CR, 47th Cong., 1st sess., 3359; Sievers, *Harrison*, 2:221–24, 231; newspaper clipping, n.d., Scrapbook No. 2, BH-LC.

28. Calhoun, *Gresham*, 74–81; Sievers, *Harrison*, 2:247–53; BH to LTM, June 11, 1884, BH-LC; A. C. Harris to WQG, June 7, 1884, WQG-LC.

29. Sievers, *Harrison*, 2:253–63; BH to WHHM, December 20, 1884, BH-Walker.

30. Sievers, *Harrison*, 2:241; Edward McPherson, *A Hand-Book of Politics for 1886* (Reprint: New York: Da Capo, 1972), 52–53, 177.

31. CR, 48th Cong., 2nd sess., 1152–56.

32. IJ, n.d.[November 1887], clipping, Scrapbook No. 2, BH-LC.

33. CR, 49th Cong., 1st sess., 2790–97; BH to D. S. Alexander, April 23, 1886, BH-LC; BH to LTM, March 27, April 2, 1886, LTM-LC.

34. BH to T. P. Keator, February 19, 1885, to E. G. Hay, May 5, 1885, to R. S. Taylor, April 9, 1886, to W. Woodward, April 20, 1886, to J. K. Gowdy, July 16, 1886, to A. M. Kennedy, July 31, 1886, Woodward to "Dear Sir," April 21, 1886, Gowdy to BH, July 16, 1886, Kennedy to BH, July 27, 1886, BH-LC.

35. IJ, September 3, 16, October 12, 1886; BH to H. E. Wells, May 1, 1886, BH-LC.

36. Justin E. Walsh, *The Centennial History of the Indiana General Assembly, 1816–1978* (Indianapolis: Indiana Historical Bureau, 1987),

203–7; *Providence Journal,* February 11, 1887; P. B. Plumb to BH, November 10, 1886, BH-LC.

3: HOOSIER IN COMMAND

1. EWH, diary, April 21, 1889, BH-Walker; *Indianapolis News,* January 5, 1886; BH to C. N. Hunter, February 6, 1885, to MWP, April 5, November 12, 1886, to J. H. Woodward, June 5, 1886, to WHHM, July 30, 1886, to E. G. Hay, November 26, 1886, BH-LC.
2. *Providence Journal,* February 11, 1887; newspaper clippings, n.d., Scrapbook No. 2, D. S. Alexander to BH, November 13, 1887, BH-LC.
3. James D. Richardson, *A Compilation of the Messages and Papers of the Presidents* (Washington, D.C.: Bureau of National Literature and Art, 1903), 8:580–91; JGB to WR, January 12, 26, 1888, WR-LC; NYTr, December 8, 1887, February 13, 1888.
4. SBE to BH, February 11, 14, 1888, J. W. Study to BH, February 1, 1888 (with BH draft reply), BH-LC; BH to SBE, February 18, 1888, SBE-WVU; LTM, "The Harrison Campaign for the Nomination in 1888," typescript, LTM-LC; JWF to WQG, February 14, 1888, WQG-LC; IJ, February 14, 1888; *South Bend Tribune,* February 14, 1888.
5. Hedges, *Speeches of Harrison,* 9–24.
6. JGB to SBE, March 1, 1888, SBE-WVU; Calhoun, *Gresham,* 92–94; SBE to BH, February 27, 1888, CSH to Russell Harrison, May 7, 1888, BH-LC.
7. LTM, "Harrison Campaign"; LTM to EWH, May 25, 1888, BH-LC; JWF to WQG, March 26, 1888, WQG-LC; IJ, June 2, 1888; LTM to SBE, February 27, 1888, SBE-WVU.
8. SBE to BH, March 31, April 6, May 2, 7, 1888, BH-LC; SBE to LTM, March 21, 26, April 7, May 8, 19, 1888, LTM-LC; SBE to WR, April 23, 1888, WR to C. F. Crocker, April 23, 1888, WR-LC; IJ, June 4, 1888; Robert D. Marcus, *Grand Old Party: Political Structure in the Gilded Age, 1880–1896* (New York: Oxford University Press, 1971), 112–14.
9. John Hay to WR, June 22, 1888, WR-LC; LTM, "The National Convention of 1888," typescript, LTM-LC; *Official Proceedings of the Republican National Convention . . . 1888* (Minneapolis: Charles W. Johnson, 1903), 108–12; Hedges, *Speeches of Harrison,* 37, 108.
10. JRM to MHM, June 13, 1888, BH-Home; *Proceedings . . . 1888,* 113–67; A. M. Jones to JS, June 21, 22, 1888, JS-LC; H. G. Burleigh to BH, June 22, 1888, BH-LC; NYT, June 23, 1888.
11. *Proceedings . . . 1888,* 177–84; Walker Blaine to Mrs. JGB, July 5, 1888, JGB-LC; Mark Hanna to JS, June 23, 1888, JS-LC.
12. JS to Warner Miller, [June 24, 1888], M. Halstead to JS, June 24, 1888, A. E. B[ateman] to JS, June 25, 1888, Hanna to JS, June 25, 1888, JS-LC; LTM to Wharton Barker, June 24, 1888, Wharton

Barker Papers, LC; LTM, "National Convention of 1888"; Sievers, *Harrison*, 2:348–49; *Proceedings . . . 1888*, 185–99, 232–33.

13. Sievers, *Harrison*, 2:353–54; Hedges, *Speeches of Harrison*, 25–27.

14. BH to WR, October 9, 1888, WR-LC; LTM, "Harrison's Speeches in 1888," typescript, LTM-LC; Homer E. Socolofsky and Allan B. Spetter, *The Presidency of Benjamin Harrison* (Lawrence, Kan.: University Press of Kansas, 1987), 11; Sievers, *Harrison*, 2:371.

15. MSD to Elizabeth Lord, [August 20, 1888], September 6, [1888], "Friday Morning," "Saturday morning," BH to MSD, August 30, October 21, November 15, 25, 1888, February 28, 1895, MLH, manuscript note, n.d., BH-Walker.

16. Edward McPherson, *A Hand-Book of Politics for 1890* (Reprint: New York: Da Capo, 1972), 33; Hedges, *Speeches of Harrison*, 25–186.

17. Affidavit of W. S. Elliott enclosed in J. C. Wheat to BH, October 7, 1888, BH-LC; Hedges, *Speeches of Harrison*, 45, 48, 61, 80, 179.

18. Republican State Central Committee, *Gen. Harrison and Labor* (n.p., [1888]); Wallace, *Life of Harrison*, 70–72, 78, 321–32; Hedges, *Speeches of Harrison*, 38–39.

19. James A. Kehl, *Boss Rule in the Gilded Age: Matt Quay of Pennsylvania* (Pittsburgh: University of Pittsburgh Press, 1981), 97; J. M. Swank to W. B. Allison, September 26, 1888, William B. Allison Papers, State Historical Society of Iowa, Des Moines; W. W. Wood to BH (with note from TCP), June 30, 1888, BH-LC; BH to WR, September 27, 1888, WR-LC; Hedges, *Speeches of Harrison*, 162–63.

20. Arthur M. Schlesinger, Jr., ed., *History of American Presidential Elections 1789–1968* (New York: Chelsea House, 1971), 2:1644–45, 1680–82.

21. WQG to N. C. Butler, October 30, 1888, Noble C. Butler Papers, Indiana Historical Society Library, Indianapolis.

22. IJ, October 8, 1888; *Indianapolis Sentinel*, October 31, 1888; LTM, "National Convention of 1888"; W. W. Dudley to BH, December 19, 1887, BH-LC.

23. IJ, November 1, 1888; LTM, "The Dudley Letter," typescript, LTM-LC; Calhoun, *Gresham*, 104; Sievers, *Harrison*, 2:417–21.

24. Sievers, *Harrison*, 2:419–20; Richard J. Jensen, *The Winning of the Midwest: Social and Political Conflict, 1888–1896* (Chicago: University of Chicago Press, 1971), 29; *Indianapolis Sentinel*, November 8, 1888.

25. William G. Shade and Ballard C. Campbell, eds., *American Presidential Campaigns and Elections* (Armonk, N.Y.: M. E. Sharpe, 2003), 2:518, 536; *Statistical History of the United States, From Colonial Times to 1970* (New York: Basic Books, 1976), 34; Albert T. Volwiler, ed., *The Correspondence between Benjamin Harrison and James G. Blaine, 1882–1893* (Philadelphia: American Philosophical Society, 1940), 41.

26. BH to MSD, November 15, 1888, BH-Walker.

4: CENTENNIAL PRESIDENT

1. J. R. Hawley to BH, December 27, 1888, BH-LC; Kehl, *Boss Rule,* 117.
2. EWH, "How Harrison Chose His Cabinet," *Leslie's Weekly,* April 19, 1919, p. 574; Allan Burton Spetter, "Harrison and Blaine: Foreign Policy, 1889–1893" (Ph.D. diss., Rutgers University, 1967), 12–16; Oscar Doane Lambert, *Stephen Benton Elkins: American Foursquare* (Pittsburgh: University of Pittsburgh Press, 1955), 126–28; Volwiler, *Correspondence between Harrison and Blaine,* 40–50.
3. LTM, "The Formation of the Cabinet," typescript, "Published in the Star of March 10, 1910," typescript, TCP to LTM, January 18, 1889, LTM-LC; BH to SBE, January 18, 1889 (copy), BFT to BH, December 31, 1888 (copy), TCP-Yale.
4. Socolofsky and Spetter, *Presidency of Harrison,* 23–25; BH to W. B. Allison, January 17, February 4, 1889, Allison to BH, January 31, 1889, BH-LC; E. G. Hay, "Benjamin Harrison: An Appreciation," typescript, Eugene Gano Hay Papers, LC; Sievers, 3:11–15.
5. Willard Warner to JS, January 10, 1889, JS-LC; A. E. Willson to BH, February 4, 1889, BH to R. B. Hayes, January 22, 1889, J. M. Harlan to BH, December 25, 1888, BH-LC.
6. LTM, "The Formation of the Cabinet"; ANB, 15:522–23, 16:469, 17:898.
7. Kehl, *Boss Rule,* 118–19; Socolofsky and Spetter, *Presidency of Harrison,* 24–27; J. M. Rusk to LTM, October 26, November 10, December 9, 13, 1888, February 20, 1889, LTM-LC.
8. Elizabeth Lord to MSD, February 25, 1889, EWH, diary, February 25, 1889, BH-Walker; Hedges, *Speeches of Harrison,* 191.
9. Sievers, *Harrison,* 3:33; EWH, diary, February 26, 28, March 1, 2, 3, 1889, Elizabeth Lord to MSD, March 25, 1889, BH-Walker; IJ, March 5, 1889.
10. Hedges, *Speeches of Harrison,* 194–203; IJ, March 5, 1889.
11. Elizabeth Lord to MSD, March 10, 25, [April 8], 1889, BH to MSD, September 28, 1889, BH-Walker.
12. BH to MSD, March 5, April 13, September 28, 1889, Elizabeth Lord to MSD, March 10, 1889, MSD to Lord, March 26, 1889, BH-Walker.
13. BH to MSD, April 13, 1889, BH-Walker; BH, *This Country of Ours* (New York: Charles Scribner's Sons, 1897),161; Michael Medved, *The Shadow Presidents* (New York: Times Books, 1979), 88–92.
14. EWH diary, April 4, June 2, 1891, BH-Walker.
15. EWH, "General Harrison's Attitude toward the Presidency," *Century Magazine* 84 (1912), 307, 309; Shelby M. Cullom, *Fifty Years of Public Service* (Chicago: A. C. McClurg and Co., 1911), 249; WHHM to EWH, March 22, 1912, Miller Letterbook, BH-Home; Hay, "Harrison"; BH, *This Country,* 112, 166, 168, 179–80; Medved, *Shadow Presidents,* 90; Sievers, *Harrison,* 3:142–43.

16. NYTr, May 1, 1889; CSH, diary, [April 30, 1889], BH-Home; Sievers, *Harrison*, 3:75.

17. Sievers, *Harrison*, 3:117–28; Donald L. McMurry, "The Bureau of Pensions during the Administration of President Harrison," *Mississippi Valley Historical Review* 13 (1926): 343–64; IJ, September 12, 13, 1889; BH to GFH, September 12, 23, 1889, GFH-MHS; Richardson, *Messages*, 9:49–50.

18. Hedges, *Speeches of Harrison*, 68–69, 108–115; Volwiler, *Correspondence between Harrison and Blaine*, 44–45, 49.

19. EWH, "Harrison in the White House," *Leslie's Weekly*, May 3, 1919, p. 685; Harriet S. Blaine Beale, ed., *Letters of Mrs. James G. Blaine* (New York: Duffield, 1908), 2:256–58; Volwiler, *Correspondence between Harrison and Blaine*, 301; JGB to HCL, July 27, 1889, Mrs. JGB to Mrs. HCL, July 27, 1889, JGB to Mrs. HCL, August 27, 1889, HCL-MHS; CSH to MHM, June 30, 1891, BH-Home.

20. Spetter, "Harrison and Blaine," 19–30; Volwiler, *Correspondence between Harrison and Blaine*, 60–61; CSH, diary, [April 30, 1889], BH-Home; Hedges, *Speeches of Harrison*, 209–11.

21. CSH to MHM, June 30, 1891, BH to CSH, September 19, 1891, BH-Home; JGB to Mrs. HCL, September 9, 1890, HCL-MHS; BH to CSH, June 25, September 22, 1891, BH-IHS.

22. Charles S. Campbell, *The Transformation of American Foreign Relations, 1865–1900* (New York: Harper and Row, 1976), 72–83; Spetter, "Harrison and Blaine," 263–72; Paul M. Kennedy, *The Samoan Tangle* (New York: Barnes and Noble, 1974), 1–97; Volwiler, *Correspondence between Harrison and Blaine*, 58, 59, 61, 63, 65, 302; Beale, *Letters of Mrs. Blaine*, 2:262–63; FRUS, 1889, 195–205, 349–64; JGB to Mrs. HCL, June 17, 1889, HCL-MHS; Richardson, *Messages*, 9:34.

23. BH to MSD, April 13, June 3, July 18, August 17, 24, September 1, 6, 16, 28, October 6, 12, November 10, 1889, BH-Walker; CSH, diary, [November–December], 1889, BH-Home; MHM to Eugie Peltz, May 29, 1890, BH-IHS.

24. MSD, White House diary, passim, MSD to CSH, n.d. [1891], with BH reply, MSD to Lizzie Parker, October 1, 12, 19, 31, November 15, 27, December 7, 1890, BH to MSD, March 28, October 19, 1891, BH-Walker; MSD to Lucretia Garfield, n.d. [1890], April 16, [1890], Lucretia Garfield Papers, LC; unidentified newspaper clippings, Scrapbook No. 50, Wm. F. Wharton to BH, [September 3, 1891] (translation in MSD's hand), JGB to BH, August 16, 1891, coded telegram with translation by MSD, BH-LC.

25. Sievers, *Harrison*, 3:103–15; Spetter, "Harrison and Blaine," 194–200; Edward P. Crapol, *James G. Blaine: Architect of Empire* (Wilmington, Del.: SR Books, 2000), 118–21; David Healy, *James G. Blaine and Latin America* (Columbia, Mo.: University of Missouri Press, 2001), 147–59.

26. Volwiler, *Correspondence between Harrison and Blaine*, 90, 302; BH to MSD, October 12, 1889, EWH, diary, November 22, 27, 30, 1889, BH-Walker.

## 5: THE BILLION-DOLLAR CONGRESS

1. BH to GFH, August 26, 1889, GFH-MHS; Volwiler, *Correspondence between Harrison and Blaine*, 77–78, 83–84.
2. Richardson, *Messages*, 9:32–58; IJ, December 4, 1889; NYTr, December 4, 1889; George Edmunds to BH, December 4, 1889, BH-LC.
3. R. Hal Williams, *Years of Decision: American Politics in the 1890s* (New York: John Wiley and Sons, 1978), 21–25.
4. Richardson, *Messages*, 9:37–39.
5. Williams, *Years of Decision*, 26–28; S. J. Peele to EWH, March 15, 1890, BH-LC; NYT, February 12, 1890.
6. House Report 1466, 51st Cong., 1st sess.
7. EWH diary, March 22, 1890, BH-Walker; Williams, *Years of Decision*, 28; CR, 51st Cong., 1st sess., 5112–13; McPherson, *1890*, 238.
8. *Annual Report of the Attorney General, 1889*, xiv–xv, xxii–xxiii; Robert M. Goldman, *"A Free Ballot and a Fair Count"* (New York: Fordham University Press, 2001), 145–68, 177–78n61.
9. Richardson, *Messages*, 9:55–56.
10. H.R. 8242, 51st Cong., 1st sess.; Richardson, *Messages*, 9:56; HCL to Anna Cabot Lodge, June 9, 15, 1890, HCL-MHS.
11. H.R. 11045 (June 19, 1890), 51st Cong., 1st sess.
12. JCS to George Farnam, May 8, 1890, JCS-LC; CR, 51st Cong., 1st sess., 6553, 6940–41; CR, 51st Cong., 2nd sess., 723; T. J. Henderson, form letter to "Dear Sir," June 26, 1890, N. P. Banks Papers, LC.
13. Richardson, *Messages*, 9:54–55; CR, 51st Cong., 1st sess., 100, 2200, 2436; McPherson, *1890*, 194; JCS to J. F. Dudley, March 16, 1890, JCS-LC.
14. Richardson, *Messages*, 9:49–50; McPherson, *1890*, 125–27; Theda Skocpol, *Protecting Soldiers and Mothers* (Cambridge, Mass.: Harvard University Press, 1992), 128; *Statistical History of the United States*, 1104, 1146.
15. Williams, *Years of Decision*, 32–33; Richardson, *Messages*, 9:43; McPherson, *1890*, 117–119; Hans B. Thorelli, *The Federal Trust Policy: Origins of an American Tradition* (Baltimore: Johns Hopkins University Press, 1955), 164–210, 371–80, 590.
16. *Proceedings of the First National Silver Convention* (St. Louis: Buxton and Skinner, 1889); LTM to EWH, November 26, 1889, BH-LC.
17. Richardson, *Messages*, 9:39–41; *Annual Report of the Secretary of the Treasury, 1889*, lx–lxxxiv.
18. EWH, diary, January 20, 1890, BH-Walker.
19. Cincinnati *Commercial-Gazette*, February 25, April 13, 1890; NYT, April 13, 15, 21, 1890; EWH, diary, March 17, 1890, BH-Walker; EWH, "Some of President Harrison's Troubles," *Leslie's Weekly*, May 17, 1919, p. 755.
20. CR, 51st Cong., 1st sess., 5652, 5814–15; F. G. Newlands to BH, June 5, 1890, BH-LC; Francis Newlands, *Mr. Newlands on Silver* (Washington: Geo. R. Gray, 1890), 14–15; IJ, June 6, 1890; McPherson, *1890*, 146.

21. CR, 51st Cong., 1st sess., 6165–83; IJ, June 19, 1890; EWH, diary, June 17, 1890, BH-Walker.
22. BH to CSH, July 13, 1890, BH-Home; IJ, June 21, 1890; EWH, diary, June 21, 24, 1890, BH to MSD, June 26, 1890, BH-Walker; CR, 51st Cong., 1st sess., 6501, 6503–6504; McPherson, *1890*, 154–55.
23. CR, 51st Cong., 1st sess., 6975–76, 6982, 7108–7109, 7226; McPherson, *1890*, 156; Clarence Johnson to William E. Chandler, July 8, 1890, William E. Chandler Papers, New Hampshire Historical Society, Concord.
24. EWH, diary, July 12, 14, 1890, BH-Walker; BH to CSH, July 13, 1890, BH-Home; IJ, July 14, 1890.
25. Senate Ex. Doc. No. 158, 51st Cong., 1st sess.; Tom Terrill, *The Tariff, Politics, and American Foreign Policy, 1874–1901* (Westport: Greenwood, 1973) 165–66; JGB to Justin Morrill, June 20, 1890, Justin Morrill Papers, LC; NYTr, June 23, 1890; P. C. Cheney to LTM, March 23, "1893" [1896], LTM-LC.
26. Volwiler, *Correspondence between Harrison and Blaine*, 109–13; NYTr, July 15, 26, 27, 1890; BH to CSH, July 13, 1890, BH-Home.
27. BH to MSD, July 27, 1890, BH-Walker; JGB to Mrs. HCL, July 20, September 6, 9, 1890, HCL-MHS; NYT, August 3, 4, 8, 9, 29, 1890; McPherson, *1890*, 16–17; NYTr, March 17, 1891; Dingley's observation is in Cheney to LTM, March 23, "1893," [1896], LTM-LC.
28. Volwiler, *Correspondence between Harrison and Blaine*, 115; BH to MSD, August 8, 16, 1890, BH-Walker; Hedges, *Speeches of Harrison*, 226–31; Kehl, *Boss Rule*, 128–33; CR, 51st Cong., 1st sess., 8355, 8422, 8440, 8466.
29. EWH, diary, August 14, 15, 1890, BH to MSD, August 16, 1890, BH-Walker; NYT, August 19, 1890; *Chicago Tribune*, August 18, 1890; IJ, August 17, 1890.
30. JGB to Mrs. HCL, August 31, 1890, HCL-MHS; *Chicago Tribune*, August 15, 16, 23, 1890; *Philadelphia Press*, August 16, 20, 1890; CR, 51st Cong., 1st sess., 8842–48, 9943, 10333; NYT, August 22, 24, 1890; signed pledge, "Washington, D.C. August 22, 1890," Eugene Hale and JCS to "My Dear Sir," August 25, 1890, GFH-MHS; EWH, diary, August 15, 21, 1890, BH-Walker.
31. JCS to E. Enos, September 6, 1890, JCS to C. H. Williams, November 19, 1890, JCS-LC; Frederick Douglass to GFH, September 2, 1890, GFH-MHS.
32. MSD to L. Parker, September 21, 1890, BH-Walker; "Telegraphic Talk at Cresson," September 1890, BH-LC.
33. Telegrams between BH and Treasury officials, September 12–17, 1890, William Windom to BH, September 18, 1890, "Telegraphic Talk at Cresson," September 1890, BH-LC; EWH to BFT, September 18, 1890, BFT-LC; IJ, September 13, 14, 1890, February 8, 1892.
34. Hedges, *Speeches of Harrison*, 231–34; IJ, June 5, 1889; September 14, 23, 1890; Sievers, *Harrison*, 3:77; Socolofsky and Spetter, *Presidency of Harrison*, 92; MSD to L. Parker, September 21, October 1 and 3, 1890, BH-Walker.

35. MSD to L. Parker, September 27 and 30, October 19, 1890, BH-Walker; Calhoun, "Caroline Lavinia Scott Harrison," 178–79.

36. EWH, diary, July 29, October 17, 1890, BH-Walker; Richardson, *Messages*, 9:44, 80–81; *Supplement to the Revised Statutes of the United States* (Washington: Government Printing Office, 1891), 794–97, 803–5; Socolofsky and Spetter, *Presidency of Harrison*, 131–36; Benjamin Franklin Cooling, *Benjamin Franklin Tracy* (Hamden: Archon, 1973), 74–78, 87–88; Spetter, "Harrison and Blaine," 43–44.

37. MSD to L. Parker, October 1, 1890, BH-Walker; IJ, October 2, 4, 7, 1890; NYTr, October 3, 1890; EWH to Edward McPherson, October 17, 22, 1890, Edward McPherson Papers, LC.

38. LTM to EWH, August 25, October 16, 1890, LTM to BH, October 29, 1890, BH to LTM, October 31, 1890, BH-LC; Hedges, *Speeches of Harrison*, 234–86.

39. Williams, *Years of Decision*, 50; BH to Howard Cale, November 17, 1890, BH to R. S. Taylor, November 29, 1890, E. F. Tibbott, diary, November 8, 1890, BH-LC.

40. SBE to WR, November 14, 1890, WR-LC; MSD to L. Parker, November 27, 1890, BH-Walker; JGB to Mrs. HCL, January 4, 1891, HCL-MHS.

41. IJ, November 11–13, 1890; SBE to WR, November 14, 1890, WR-LC; Elmus Wicker, *Banking Panics of the Gilded Age* (Cambridge: Cambridge University Press, 2000), 45–47; MSD to L. Parker, November 15, 20, December 7, 1890, BH-Walker.

42. BH to JSC, December 2, 1890, BH-LC; Richardson, *Messages*, 9:107–29.

43. BH to CSH, December 4, 1890, BH-IHS; MSD to L. Parker, December 7, 1890, BH-Walker; NYTr, December 8, 1890; John Wanamaker to BH, December 13, 1890, BH-LC; NYT, December 14, 15, 1890.

44. IJ, December 5, 16, 18, 24, 1890; NYT, December 15–18, 1890; CR, 51st Cong., 2nd sess., 873, 875; Thomas Upchurch, *Legislating Racism* (Lexington: University Press of Kentucky, 2004), 129–50.

45. Richardson, *Messages*, 9:45, 117; BH to secretary of war, October 31, November 13, 1890, BH to secretary of the interior, November 13, December 3, 20, 1890, Redfield Proctor to Nelson Miles, November 28, 1890, Miles to John M. Schofield, December 20, 1890, T. J. Morgan to secretary of the interior, December 24, 1890, BH-LC; Robert Utley, *The Indian Frontier, 1846–1890* (Albuquerque: University of New Mexico Press, 2003), 243–44.

46. Schofield to Miles, January 8, 1891, BH to D. F. Royer, January 8, 1891, BH-LC; *Wounded Knee Massacre: Hearings before the Committee on the Judiciary, United States Senate* (Washington: Government Printing Office, 1976), 117–39; NYT, February 13, 1891; Robert Utley, *The Last Days of the Sioux Nation* (New Haven: Yale University Press, 1963), 244–49.

47. BH to Mrs. H. S. Howell, January 19, 1891, "Mem[orandum] by the President for a message in re Sioux troubles," "The President to the

Sioux Indians lately on the war Path—In the East Room, Feb[ruar]y 12, 1891," BH-LC; Richardson, *Messages*, 9:173, 174, 176–78.

48. HCL to Anna Cabot Lodge, December 8, 1890, HCL-MHS; NYT, December 30, 1890; NYTr, January 3, 6, 1891; CR, 51st Cong., 2nd sess., 912–13; Edward McPherson, *A Hand-Book of Politics for 1892* (Reprint: New York: Da Capo, 1972), 27, 30, 219; Harrison Kelley to Mr. and Mrs. Albion W. Tourgée, January 1, 1891, Albion W. Tourgée Papers, Chautauqua County Historical Society, Westfield, New York; John R. Lambert, Jr., *Arthur Pue Gorman* (Baton Rouge: Louisiana State University Press, 1953), 159.

49. CR, 51st Cong., 2nd sess., 1323; J. P. Jones to Mrs. Jones, January 15, 1891, John P. Jones Papers, Huntington Library, Pasadena, Calif.; IJ, January 23, 29, 30, February 7, 1891; NYT, February 23, 1891; NYTr, March 17, 1891.

50. CR, 51st Cong., 2nd sess., 1324, 1564–68, 1651–55, 1738–40; JSC to BH, January 15, 1891, BH-LC; JCS to J. M. Bundy, January 27, 1891, JCS-LC; NYTr, March 17, 1891; William M. Stewart, *Reminiscences* (New York: Neale Publishing Company, 1908), 310.

51. Hedges, *Speeches of Harrison*, 305, 543; Richardson, *Messages*, 9:210–11, 332; *Public Papers and Addresses of Benjamin Harrison* (Washington: Government Printing Office, 1893), 294; IJ, June 1, 1892. See also Edward Frantz, "A March of Triumph? Benjamin Harrison's Southern Tour and the Limits of Racial and Regional Reconciliation," IMH (December 2004), 293–320.

52. *Supplement to the Revised Statutes*, 905–907, 947; NYTr, March 17, 1891; Socolofsky and Spetter, *Presidency of Harrison*, 69–73.

53. *Statistical History of the United States*, 1081–82; HCL to Anna Cabot Lodge, March 8, 1891, HCL-MHS; NYTr, March 17, 1891; IJ, March 5, 1891.

## 6: DIPLOMACY AND DEFEAT

1. BH to Howard Cale, February 28, 1891, BH-LC; CSH, notes on Tour of the President to the Pacific Coast, 1891, BH-IHS; MSD, diary, February 10, 1891, BH to MSD, March 28, 1891, BH-Walker.

2. Hedges, *Speeches of Harrison*, 289–490; *Tour of the President, to the Pacific Coast, April 14th to May 16th 1891—Itinerary*, BH-Home; MSD, notes on "Trip to California—President's Trip," BH-Walker; BH to Clem Studebaker, May 18, 1891, BH-LC.

3. Richardson, *Messages*, 9:265–69, 312; Spetter, "Harrison and Blaine," 64–81; Healy, *James G. Blaine*, 168–79.

4. Volwiler, *Correspondence between Harrison and Blaine*, 191, 193–96, 199, 201–3, 241–42; Spetter, "Harrison and Blaine," 81–93.

5. Richardson, *Messages*, 9:312–13; Calhoun, *Gresham*, 138–39.

6. Richardson, *Messages*, 9:199–200, 322–23; David M. Pletcher, *The Diplomacy of Trade and Investment* (Columbia, Mo.: University of Missouri Press, 1998), 275–77.

7. *Supplement to the Revised Statutes,* 905–7; Richardson, *Messages,* 9:323–24.

8. Richardson, *Messages,* 9:35–36, 109, 188–90, 317; Pletcher, *Diplomacy of Trade,* 283–90; Joseph A. Fry, *John Tyler Morgan and the Search for Southern Autonomy* (Knoxville: University of Tennessee Press, 1992), 98–100.

9. Richardson, *Messages,* 9:10; Rayford W. Logan, *The Diplomatic Relations of the United States with Haiti, 1776–1891* (Chapel Hill: University of North Carolina Press, 1941), 411–57; William S. McFeely, *Frederick Douglass* (New York: W. W. Norton, 1991), 338–56; John W. Blassingame and John R. McKivigan, eds., *Frederick Douglass Papers,* Series 1 (New Haven: Yale University Press, 1979–1992), 5:513.

10. Pletcher, *Diplomacy of Trade,* 302–3; Volwiler, *Correspondence between Harrison and Blaine,* 169, 173–74.

11. BH to WR, July 21, October 21, 1891, WR to BH, October 9, 1891, BH-LC; Volwiler, *Correspondence between Harrison and Blaine,* 170, 173–74.

12. FRUS, 1894, Appendix, 350–52 and passim; Julius Pratt, *Expansionists of 1898* (Baltimore: Johns Hopkins University Press, 1936), 47–48; Volwiler, *Correspondence between Harrison and Blaine,* 190–91, 206, 211–12; Richardson, *Messages,* 9:316.

13. Richardson, *Messages,* 9:308; Robert L. Beisner, *From the Old Diplomacy to the New, 1865–1900* (Arlington Heights, Ill.: AHM Publishing Corporation, 1975), 86.

14. Spetter, "Harrison and Blaine," 170–79; Sievers, *Harrison,* 3:183–90; H. Remsen Whitehouse to JGB, March 13, 14, 17, 19, 1892, BH, draft of Wharton to Whitehouse, March 16, 1892 [March 13, 1892], Wharton to Whitehouse, March 16, 1892, BH-LC; Volwiler, *Correspondence between Harrison and Blaine,* 141–142, 149, 152, 158, 192–93, 202, 206, 246–51; FRUS, 1891, 727–28.

15. Patrick Egan to William F. Wharton, October 19, 1891, W. S. Schley to secretary of the navy, October 22, 1891, BH-LC; Joyce Goldberg, *The Baltimore Affair* (Lincoln: University of Nebraska Press, 1986), 1–19, 32–56. This account of the *Baltimore* affair relies heavily on Goldberg, although I do not agree with her version in all particulars. See also Healy, *James G. Blaine,* 205–34.

16. Wharton to Egan, October 23, 1891, FRUS, 1891, 196–97; BH, draft of note to Egan, October 23, 1891, BH-LC; Richardson, *Messages,* 9:183–86; Goldberg, *Baltimore Affair,* 118–22.

17. FRUS, 1891, 267–69; Goldberg, *Baltimore Affair,* 100–101, 122; JWF to BH, January 12, 1892, A. A. Adee to EWH, January 13, 1892, BH-LC; EWH, diary, January 16, 1892, BH-Walker.

18. Goldberg, *Baltimore Affair,* 93–99, 118; BH, "Mem[orandum] prepared for Cabinet meeting Tuesday Jan[uar]y 19th [1892]," "Original draft—Jan[uar]y 21/92," BH-LC; FRUS, 1891, 307–8; Richardson, *Messages,* 9:215–26.

19. FRUS, 1891, 309–13; John A. Garraty, *Henry Cabot Lodge* (New York: Knopf, 1965), 148–49; Volwiler, *Correspondence between Harrison and Blaine*, 238–39; Richardson, *Messages*, 9:227; Goldberg, *Baltimore Affair*, 131.
20. Charles S. Campbell, Jr., "The Anglo-American Crisis in the Bering Sea, 1890–1891," *Mississippi Valley Historical Review* 48 (December 1961): 393–403; Campbell, "The Bering Sea Settlements of 1892," *Pacific Historical Review* 32 (November 1963): 347–53; BH, "Behring Sea Controversy," (draft), December 15, 1890, BH-LC; FRUS, 1891, 500, 614–19.
21. Campbell, "Anglo-American Crisis," 403–13; Volwiler, *Correspondence between Harrison and Blaine*, 144–47, 151–52, 154–55, 156–57, 159, 161; FRUS, 1891, 568–73; EWH, diary, June 3, 4, 6, 9, 11, 13, 1891, BH-Walker.
22. Campbell, "Bering Sea Settlements," 357–65; Volwiler, *Correspondence between Harrison and Blaine*, 242–43, 245–46, 251–59; BH, draft of note from Wharton to Julian Pauncefote, March 22, 1892, E. F. Tibbott, diary, March 22, 1892, E. J. Phelps to BH, March 10, 19, 1892, BH to Phelps, March 17, 1892, Wharton to BH, March 16, 1892, JWF to BH, March 19, 1892, BH-LC; FRUS, 1891, 619–37.
23. Volwiler, *Correspondence between Harrison and Blaine*, 147–48; IJ, May 12, 1891; EWH, diary, June 14, 1891, BH-Walker; CSH to MHM, June 23, 30, 1891, BH to CSH, September 19, 1891, BH-Home; BH to CSH, June 25, September 22, 1891, BH-IHS.
24. CSH to JRM, March 8, 1891, BH-Home; BH to Jesse Spaulding, September 29, 1891, BH to Andrew Carnegie, October 5, 1891, LTM to EWH, July 31, 1891, BH-LC.
25. Stanley P. Hirshson, "James S. Clarkson Versus Benjamin Harrison, 1891–1893: A Political Saga," *Iowa Journal of History* 58 (1960): 220; IJ, February 8, 1891; LTM to EWH, July 28, 30, 31, August 10, 1891, BH-LC.
26. S. J. Peele to LTM, August 10, 12, 20, 27, 1891, LTM to EWH, August 28, 1891, BH-LC; Hedges, *Speeches of Harrison*, 493–549.
27. LTM to EWH, August 29, September 3, 1891, JSC to EWH, September 18, 1891, JSC to BH, September 26, 1891, BH-LC; EWH to LTM, September 1, 4, 1891, LTM-LC; BH to CSH, September 19, 1891, BH-Home, JGB to SBE, August 30, 1891, SBE-WVU; Lambert, *Elkins*, 139.
28. IJ, June 18, August 20, September 17, 1891; NYTr, July 2, September 10, 1891.
29. Joseph Medill to JGB, November 30, 1891, JGB-LC; David Saville Muzzey, *James G. Blaine: A Political Idol of Other Days* (New York: Dodd, Mead, 1934), 469–70; Peele to EWH, January 9, 11, 20, 22, February 3, 1892, BH to Louis Hartman, January 14, 1892, BH-LC.
30. Medill to JGB, November 30, 1891, JGB-LC; IJ, February 8, 1892; Charles Foster to BH, February 8, 1892, BH-LC; Volwiler, *Correspondence between Harrison and Blaine*, 245, 273–76, 278–79, 291–93.

31. Peele to EWH, March 5, 11, 1892, BH to J. K. Gowdy, March 16, 24, 1892, E. H. Conger to EWH, March 18, 1892, W. Livingstone to EWH, April 14, 1892, R. G. Evans to EWH, May 6, 1892, BH-LC.

32. D. S. Alexander to BH, May 4, 1892, BH to Felix Angus, May 7, 1892, BH to Alexander, May 7, 1892, P. C. Cheney to BH, May 9, 1892, BH to Cheney, May 10, 1892, BH-LC.

33. NYT, May 20, 21, 23, 24, 25, 1892; Marcus, *Grand Old Party*, 169–70.

34. LTM, "Harrison Prior to the National Convention of 1892," typescript, and "The Minneapolis Convention of June 7th to 10th, 1892," typescript, EWH, diary, May 23, 24, 1892, BH-Walker; IJ, May 25, 26, 29, 30, 31, June 2, 1892; NYT, May 26, 1892; W. J. Sewall to LTM, May 27, 1892, Horace Porter to LTM, May 27, 1892, Perry S. Heath to LTM, May 30, 1892, LTM-LC; LTM to BFT, May 30, 1892, BFT-LC.

35. Volwiler, *Correspondence between Harrison and Blaine*, 288; IJ, June 5, 8, 1892; LTM to EWH, July 30, 1891, BH-LC; EWH, diary, June 4, 1892, MSD, diary, June 4, 1892, BH-Walker.

36. IJ, June 5, 8, 9, 1892; LTM, "Minneapolis Convention," BH-Walker.

37. IJ, June 10, 1892; LTM, "Minneapolis Convention," BH-Walker; E. F. Tibbott, diary, June 9, 1892, BH-LC.

38. *Proceedings of the Tenth Republican National Convention . . . 1892* (Minneapolis: Harrison and Smith, 1892), 113–19; BH to BFT, May 5, 1896, BFT-LC.

39. MSD, diary, June 11 [10], 1892, BH-Walker; BH to John B. Elam, June 16, 1892, "16" [M. M. Estee] to Halford, June 11, 1892, BH-LC.

40. Williams, *Years of Decision*, 53–57.

41. C. M. Depew to BH, June 21, 1892, BH-LC; Michael J. Devine, *John W. Foster: Politics and Diplomacy in the Imperial Era, 1873–1917* (Athens, Ohio: Ohio University Press, 1981), 49–50; WR to BH, August 5, 1892, BH to EWH, August 20, 1892, BH-LC.

42. BH to G. M. Dodge, June 13, 1892, BH to Depew, June 27, 1892, EWH [BH draft] to JCS, July 13, 1892, Philetus Sawyer [BH draft] to H. C. Payne, July 13, 1892, BH to WR, July 19, 1892, T. H. Carter to EWH, November 1, 1892, BH-LC; George Knoles, *The Presidential Campaign and Election of 1892* (Stanford: Stanford University Press, 1942), 122–25.

43. BH to MSD, April 8, 1892, BH-Walker; BH to G. A. Pierce, May 21, June 21, 1892, to C. B. Harrison, May 21, 1892, to J. F. Kenna, May 23, 1892, to J. B. Elam, June 2, 1892, to MWP, June 15, 1892, to Mrs. Russell Harrison, June 16, 1892, to F. W. Chase, June 21, 1892, to Mrs. Bettie Harrison, July 21, 1892, to R. B. F. Peirce, July 29, 1892, BH-LC; MSD to Mrs. Russell Harrison, July 28, 1892, BH to MHM, July 30, 1892, BH-Home.

44. WR to BH, August 6, 1892, BH to WR, August 8, 1892, Frank Hiscock to BH, August 9, 1892, BH to TCP, August 17, 1892, TCP to BH, August 22, 1892, BH-LC; EWH, diary, August 31, 1892, BH-Walker; IJ, September 1, 29, 1892; NYTr, September 5, 1892.

45. BH to William Brookfield, August 19, 1892, BH to WR, August 27, 1892, Charles Foster to BH, August 31, September 18, 1892, BH to Foster, September 18, 1892, WHHM to BH, September 3, 1892, BH to WHHM, September 9, 1892, C. H. Aldrich to BH, September 10, 1892, BH-LC; EWH, diary, August 31, 1892, BH-Walker; IJ, September 1, 4, 10, 17, 1892; Richardson, *Messages*, 9:330.

46. Socolofsky and Spetter, *Presidency of Harrison*, 74–75; Roger Daniels, *Not Like Us* (Chicago: Ivan R. Dee, 1997), 44–45; IJ, September 4, 1892; Carter to BH, September 3, 1892, BH-LC. In his message to the regular session of Congress after the election, Harrison did call for further quarantine legislation. He also acknowledged the economic impact of immigration, citing "a duty to our own people, and especially to our working people . . . to check the too great flow of immigration now coming by further limitations." Richardson, *Messages*, 9:330.

47. IJ, September 6, 1892; Carter to BH, September 3, 1892, Russell Harrison to BH, September 9, 1892, BH-LC.

48. *Appletons' Annual Cyclopaedia and Register of Important Events of the Year 1892* (New York: D. Appleton and Company, 1893), 259–61; Norman B. Willey to BH, June 26, 1892, BH to Willey, July 4, 1892, WHHM to BH, July 11, 1892, EWH to BH, July 12, 1892, BH to secretary of war, July 12, 1892, BH-LC.

49. EWH, diary, July 23, 1892, BH-Walker; WR to BH, August 4, 1892, with enclosure, BH-LC; BH to WR, August 11, 1892, WR-LC.

50. Williams, *Years of Decision*, 65; Bingham Duncan, *Whitelaw Reid* (Athens, Ga.: University of Georgia Press, 1975), 153–54, 161; Edward F. McSweeney, *The Arch Enemy of Labor* (New York: Labor Educational Bureau, [1892]).

51. Williams, *Years of Decision*, 67–68; CR, 52nd Cong., 1st sess., 2543–55, 3439; IJ, April 23, 27, 1892; G. R. Peck to EWH, August 24, 1892, BH-LC.

52. *Proceedings . . . 1892*, 133–44.

53. IJ, September 15, 22, 1892.

54. Williams, *Years of Decision*, 64; IJ, September 7, October 3, 5, 15, 1892; JGB, "The Presidential Election of 1892," *North American Review* 155 (1892): 513–25; LTM to EWH, October 11, 1892, BH-LC; MHM to JRM, October 12, 1892, BH-Home.

55. IJ, October 25–29, 1892; BH to W. O. Bradley, November 16, 1892, BH-LC; EWH, diary, October 31, 1892, BH-Walker.

56. *Appletons' . . . 1892*, 128, 370, 490, 754, 827–28; Shade and Campbell, *American Presidential Campaigns* 2:552; Jensen, *Winning of the Midwest*, 159–61; Socolofsky and Spetter, *Presidency of Harrison*, 41–42; C. C. Shayne to EWH, November 10, 1892, BH-LC.

57. See correspondence in BH-LC, November 1892, passim.

58. Royal Cortissoz, *Life of Whitelaw Reid* (New York: Charles Scribner's Sons, 1921), 2:188; BH to C. N. Bliss, November 14, 1892, to Bradley, November 16, 1892, to Clem Studebaker, November 16, 1892, to

T. W. Palmer, November 19, 1892, to S. N. Chambers, November 19, 1892, BH-LC.

59. BH to Bradley, November 16, 1892, to G. A. Pierce, November 16, 1892, BH-LC; Richardson, *Messages*, 9:306–332.

60. Richardson, *Messages*, 9:348–49; Devine, *Foster*, 61–71.

7: THE CURTAIN IS DOWN

1. BH to EWH, March 12, 1893, to Thomas Ryan, March 9, 1893, to T. H. Carter, April 15, 1893, to D. S. Alexander, May 4, 1893, BH-LC; BH to MSD, March 7, 1893, BH-Walker.

2. BH to JRM, April 8, 14, May 9, 1893, MHM to JRM, "Thursday Night," [May 18, 1893], BH-Home; BH to MSD, March 7, April 3, 10, 24, 1893, BH-Walker.

3. MHM to JRM, November 29, 1892, "Thursday Night" [May 18, 1893], Bernard Batty to JRM, January 24, May 16, 1938, January 22, 1941, JRM to Batty, January 13, 1941, JRM to Josephine Kneip, January 29, 1941, BH-Home; untitled memorandum, February 15, 1901, George B. Cortelyou Papers, LC; MSD, diary, passim, CSH to MSD, June 25, 1891, BH to Lizzie Parker, May 29, 1893, BH to MSD, September 1, 1893, BH-Walker.

4. Sievers, *Harrison*, 3:255–56, 259; BH to MSD, April 27, November 12, 19, 1893, BH-Walker; Calhoun, *Gresham*, 146–54.

5. BH to MSD, April 24, 27, November 8, 1893, February 24, 1894, BH-Walker; *New York Mail and Express*, June 30, 1893; BH to LTM, August 24, 1893, LTM-LC; BH to EWH, August 19, 1893, BH-LC; IJ, November 9, 1893.

6. BH to MSD, October 2, December 3, 1893, BH-Walker.

7. BH, *Views of an Ex-President*, comp. Mary Lord Harrison (Indianapolis: Bowen-Merrill Company, 1901), 1–184; BH to MSD, March 6, 18, April 14, 29, June 2, 23, 24, 1894, BH-Walker.

8. BH to MSD, April 14, 1894, BH-Walker; IJ, September 26, October 4, 13, 14, 19, 20, 21, 1894; BH, *Views*, 388–418.

9. IJ, November 8, 1894; BH to MSD, November 15, 1894, BH-Walker.

10. BH to MSD, February 3, 28, March 5, 6, 8, 9, 1895, BH to Lizzie Parker, March 17, 1895, BH-Walker; BH to MHM, March 7, 1895, MHM to JRM, "Saturday Morning" [March 9, 1895], March 17, 1895, "Wednesday Morning" [March 27, 1895], BH-Home; Sievers, *Harrison*, 3:259.

11. BH to MSD, May 5, June 23, 25, 29, September 19, December 17, 30, 1895, March 4, 1896, BH-Walker; BH, *This Country*, i, 159.

12. BH to MSD, June 30, July 9, November 25, December 23, 1895, January 22, 1896, BH-Walker; *New York World*, January 21, 1896.

13. WR to SBE, January 4, 1896, SBE to WR, January 23, 1896, WR-LC; IJ, January 29, February 4, 1896.

14. MHM to JRM, February 25, 1896, BH-Home; BH to MSD, "Monday night" [February 10, 1896], March 6, 7, 8, 9, 12, 14, 16, 18, 19, 21, 22, 24, 26, 30, 1896, BH-Walker; Sievers, *Harrison*, 3:257.

15. BH to BFT, May 5, 1896, BFT-LC; BH to WHHM, August 16, 1896, BH-Home; BH, *Views*, 426–53; BH to Lizzie Parker, October 9, 1896, BH to MLH, October 20, 1896, BH-Walker.
16. Sievers, *Harrison*, 3:265–69.
17. BH, *Views*, 483; BH to R. W. Gilder, May 20, 1898, Morris Ross to BH, May 20, 1898 (with enclosure, "Former President Harrison"), BH-LC; BH to R. S. Taylor, October 19, 1898, BH-Home.
18. Sievers, *Harrison*, 3:269–74; BH to WHHM, September 28, October 7, 1899, BH to William E. Dodge, January 15, 1900, BH-LC.
19. Statement to press, March 3, 1900, "Interview with General Harrison," BH-LC; BH to WHHM, August 29, September 6, 18, 28, 1900, BH-Home; BH to JWF, March 10, 1900, BH-Walker; NYT, March 9, 31, 1900.
20. BH, *Views*, 338–57, 363, 500, 508–9; BH to P. S. Kennedy, January 5, 1901, BH-LC.
21. E. F. Tibbott to LTM, March 9, 1901, LTM-LC; "It has been my desire . . . ," memorandum by MLH, March 13, 1903, BH-Walker; Richardson, *Messages*, 10:320.

# Milestones

---

1833 Born at North Bend, Ohio, on August 20

1840 Grandfather William Henry Harrison elected president

1852 Graduates from Miami University, Oxford, Ohio; begins reading law with Bellamy Storer in Cincinnati

1853 Marries Caroline Lavinia Scott

1854 Admitted to bar; moves to Indianapolis and commences law practice

1857 Elected Indianapolis city attorney

1860 Elected reporter of Indiana Supreme Court; serves 1861–62

1862–65 Colonel of Seventieth Regiment of Indiana Volunteers

1864 Reelected reporter of Indiana Supreme Court; serves 1865–69

1865 Breveted brigadier general

1872 Loses Republican gubernatorial nomination

1876 Replaces Republican nominee for governor; loses general election

1877 Active on Committee of Public Safety during Great Railroad Strike

1880 Considered a dark-horse candidate for Republican presidential nomination

1881–87 United States senator from Indiana

1884 Potential Indiana favorite son for Republican presidential nomination

1887  Loses bid for reelection to the Senate

1888  Elected president

1889–91  Fifty-first Congress passes landmark legislation including McKinley Tariff Act, Sherman Silver Purchase Act, Sherman Anti-Trust Act, and Forest Reserve Act

1889  Berlin Conference: United States creates Samoan Condominium with Germany and Great Britain

1889–90  Pan-American Conference

1890  Republicans sustain heavy losses in midterm congressional elections

1891  New Orleans lynching damages relations with Italy; fracas in Valparaiso sparks crisis with Chile

1892  Anglo-American treaty sets arbitration of Bering Sea fur seal dispute

Homestead strike and other labor unrest

Death of Caroline Harrison in late October

Harrison loses presidency to Grover Cleveland

1893  Revolution in Hawaii leads to proposal for annexation

1893–1901  Practices law in Indianapolis

1896  Marries Mary Scott Lord Dimmick

1898–99  Represents Venezuela in arbitration of British Guiana boundary dispute

1901  Dies in Indianapolis on March 13

# Selected Bibliography

Beale, Harriet S. Blaine, ed. *Letters of Mrs. James G. Blaine.* 2 vols. New York: Duffield, 1908.

*Benjamin Harrison Memorial.* House Document No. 154, 77th Cong., 1st sess.

Calhoun, Charles W. "Caroline Lavinia Scott Harrison." In *American First Ladies: Their Lives and Their Legacy,* edited by Lewis L. Gould, 2nd ed. New York: Routledge, 2001, pp. 171–81.

———. *Gilded Age Cato: The Life of Walter Q. Gresham.* Lexington: University Press of Kentucky, 1988.

Campbell, Charles S., Jr. "The Anglo-American Crisis in the Bering Sea, 1890–1891." *Mississippi Valley Historical Review* 48 (December 1961): 393–414.

———. "The Bering Sea Settlements of 1892." *Pacific Historical Review* 32 (November 1963): 347–67.

Crapol, Edward P. *James G. Blaine: Architect of Empire.* Wilmington, Del.: SR Books, 2000.

Devine, Michael J. *John W. Foster: Politics and Diplomacy in the Imperial Era, 1873–1917.* Athens: Ohio University Press, 1981.

Goldberg, Joyce S. *The Baltimore Affair.* Lincoln: University of Nebraska Press, 1986.

Harrison, Benjamin. *This Country of Ours.* New York: Charles Scribner's Sons, 1897.

———. *Views of an Ex-President.* Compiled by Mary Lord Harrison. Indianapolis: Bowen-Merrill Company, 1901.

Healy, David. *James G. Blaine and Latin America.* Columbia: University of Missouri Press, 2001.

Hedges, Charles, comp. *Speeches of Benjamin Harrison.* New York: United States Book Company, 1892.

Jensen, Richard J. *The Winning of the Midwest: Social and Political Conflict, 1888–1896.* Chicago: University of Chicago Press, 1971.

Kehl, James A. *Boss Rule in the Gilded Age: Matt Quay of Pennsylvania.* Pittsburgh: University of Pittsburgh Press, 1981.

Lambert, Oscar Doane. *Stephen Benton Elkins: American Foursquare.* Pittsburgh: University of Pittsburgh Press, 1955.

Marcus, Robert D. *Grand Old Party: Political Structure in the Gilded Age, 1880–1896.* New York: Oxford University Press, 1971.

McPherson, Edward. *A Hand-Book of Politics.* Washington, 1872–94. Reprint edition. New York: Da Capo, 1972.

Medved, Michael. *The Shadow Presidents.* New York: Times Books, 1979.

Muzzey, David Saville. *James G. Blaine: A Political Idol of Other Days.* New York: Dodd, Mead, 1934.

*Official Proceedings of the Republican National Convention . . . 1888.* Minneapolis: Charles W. Johnson, 1903.

Pletcher, David M. *The Diplomacy of Trade and Investment: American Economic Expansion in the Hemisphere.* Columbia: University of Missouri Press, 1998.

*Proceedings of the Tenth Republican National Convention . . . 1892.* Minneapolis: Harrison and Smith, 1892.

Richardson, James D. *A Compilation of the Messages and Papers of the Presidents.* Washington, D.C.: Bureau of National Literature and Art, 1903.

Shade, William G., and Ballard C. Campbell, eds. *American Presidential Campaigns and Elections.* 3 vols. Armonk, N.Y.: M. E. Sharpe, 2003.

Sievers, Harry J. *Benjamin Harrison.* 3 vols. Vols. 1 and 2: New York: University Publishers, 1952, 1959. Vol. 3: Indianapolis: Bobbs-Merrill, 1968.

Socolofsky, Homer E., and Allan B. Spetter. *The Presidency of Benjamin Harrison.* Lawrence: University Press of Kansas, 1987.

Spetter, Allan Burton. "Harrison and Blaine: Foreign Policy, 1889–1893." Ph.D. diss., Rutgers University, 1967.

Upchurch, Thomas Adams. *Legislating Racism: The Billion Dollar Congress and the Birth of Jim Crow.* Lexington: University Press of Kentucky, 2004.

Volwiler, Albert T., ed. *The Correspondence between Benjamin Harrison and James G. Blaine, 1882–1893.* Philadelphia: American Philosophical Society, 1940.

Wallace, Lew. *Life of Gen. Ben Harrison.* Philadelphia: Hubbard Brothers, 1888.

Williams, R. Hal. *Years of Decision: American Politics in the 1890s.* New York: John Wiley and Sons, 1978.

# Acknowledgments

I have incurred many debts in researching this book. I can never adequately thank Ben and Sue Walker, who generously opened their home to me and gave me unlimited access to their collection of Harrison family papers. These papers afforded me new insight into hitherto obscure or unknown elements of Benjamin Harrison's personality. I deeply appreciate the Walkers' many kindnesses to me.

At the President Benjamin Harrison Home in Indianapolis, Phyllis Geeslin and Jennifer Capps offered me the run of the house and its impressive collection of Harrison manuscripts. Their intimate knowledge of the twenty-third president and his family helped me solve many a riddle in the story. The Manuscript Division of the Library of Congress is the principal repository for the papers of Harrison and many of his political associates. Jeff Flannery in the division's reading room readily and cheerfully drew on his encyclopedic knowledge of the division's holdings to answer my every query. Ed Schamel of the Center for Legislative Archives of the National Archives performed a similar service in my quest for records related to the Fifty-first Congress.

Librarians elsewhere ably facilitated my research. These include the staffs at the Indiana Historical Society, the Indiana State Library, the Massachusetts Historical Society, the New Hampshire Historical Society, the Huntington Library, the Rutherford B. Hayes

Presidential Center, the West Virginia University Library, and the Yale University Library, among others. I am also grateful to the efficient staff of the Inter-Library Loan Office of Joyner Library at East Carolina University.

Fellow historians have also aided this enterprise. No one was more generous than Lewis L. Gould, who never hesitated to send research materials and encouragement my way. Ed Crapol and Hal Williams shared with me their deep understanding of James G. Blaine. Previous authorities on Harrison have also influenced my work: George W. Geib, Harry J. Sievers, Allan B. Spetter, and Homer E. Socolofsky. In addition, although they may not fully realize it, I have been helped in a variety of ways by Roger D. Bridges, Ari Hoogenboom and Olive Hoogenboom, H. Wayne Morgan, Allan Peskin, and Mark Wahlgren Summers. Needless to say, I alone am responsible for what I have written.

I wish to thank series editor Arthur Schlesinger, Jr., for inviting me to write this book and for his thoughtful reading of the manuscript. Robin Dennis at Times Books has been a superb editor, not least for her toleration of an author with tendencies toward the obsessive-compulsive.

I am grateful to Michael Palmer, chair of the History Department at East Carolina University, and my departmental colleagues, especially Tony Papalas, for their support and encouragement.

Lastly, I wish to thank my dear wife and daughter, Bonnie and Elizabeth. I much appreciate their patient indulgence of my irksome propensity to invoke some tidbit about Benjamin Harrison in just about any context or circumstance.

# INDEX

# ABOUT THE AUTHOR

CHARLES W. CALHOUN is a professor of history at East Carolina University. A former National Endowment for the Humanities fellow, Calhoun is the author or editor of four books, including *The Gilded Age*, and a member of the editorial board of the *Journal of the Gilded Age and Progressive Era*. He lives in Greenville, North Carolina.